Montana Bucket List Adventure Guide

Explore 100 Offbeat Destinations You Must Visit!

Edward Horne

Canyon Press
canyon@purplelink.org

Please consider writing a review!
Just visit: purplelink.org/review

ISBN: 978-1-957590-08-0

FREE BONUS

Discover 31 Incredible Places You Can
Visit Next! Just Go to:

purplelink.org/travel

Table of Contents

How to Use This Book... 1

About Montana 3

    Landscape and Climate 4

Arlee

    The Garden of One Thousand Buddhas........................ 7

Babb

    Apikuni Falls.. 8

    Bowman Lake 9

    Cracker Lake Trail 10

    Hidden Falls 11

    Iceberg Lake.. 12

    Lake Josephine... 13

    Saint Mary Falls... 14

    Siyeh Pass Trail.. 15

    Stoney Indian Pass 16

    Swiftcurrent Lake... 17

Bigfork

    Bigfork Art & Cultural Center 18

Big Sandy

    White Cliffs.. 19

Big Sky

    Big Sky Resort & Bridger Bowl Ski Area 20

    Ousel Falls Park 21

Billings

    Alberta Bair Theatre 22

    Billings Studio Theatre 23

    Centennial Park.. 24

DanWalt Gardens...25

Dehler Park 26

Four Dances Recreation Area 27

Lake Elmo State Park...28

MetraPark..29

Montana Audubon Conservation Education Center 30

Moss Mansion Museum..31

Pictograph Cave State Park...32

Reef Indoor Water Park 33

Riverfront Park..34

The Rimrocks...35

Western Heritage Center...36

Yellowstone Art Museum..37

Yellowstone Cellars & Winery.....................................38

Yellowstone County Museum.......................................39

ZooMontana...40

Bozeman
American Computer & Robotics Museum 41

Bozeman Hot Springs 42

Bridger Bowl...43

College "M" Hiking Trail 44

Custer Gallatin National Forest 45

Gallatin History Museum..46

Gallatin River..47

Hyalite Canyon Recreation Area 48

Little Bighorn Battlefield National Monument............49

Montana Grizzly Encounter...50

Potosi Hot Springs 51

Spotted Bear Ranch.. 52

The Museum of the Rockies 53

Butte
Ringing Rocks.. 54

The World Museum of Mining........................... 55

Coram
Amazing Fun Center.. 56

Deer Lodge
Grant-Kohrs Ranch National Historic Site 57

Dillon
Big Hole National Battlefield 58

Fort Smith
Bighorn Canyon Recreation Area........................ 59

Gardiner
Grizzly and Wolf Discovery Center 60

Hebgen Lake 61

Quake Lake 62

Yellowstone National Park 63

Glendive
Makoshika State Park 64

Great Falls
Benton Lake National Wildlife Refuge 65

C.M. Russell Museum 66

Giant Springs State Park................................... 67

Paris Gibson Square Museum of Art 68

River's Edge Trail.. 69

The History Museum 70

Hamilton

Blodgett Canyon 71

Helena

Canyon Ferry Lake 72

Cathedral of Saint Helena 73

ExplorationWorks 74

Gates of the Mountains Wilderness 75

Helena National Forest 76

Holter Museum of Art 77

Montana Historical Society 78

Montana State Capitol 79

Mount Helena City Park 80

Original Governor's Mansion 81

Reeder's Alley 82

Spring Meadow Lake State Park 83

Jefferson City

Tizer Botanic Gardens & Arboretum 84

Kalispell

Artemis Acres Paint Horse Ranch 85

Flathead Lake 86

Hockaday Museum of Art 87

Swan Lake 88

Wild Horse Island State Park 89

Lewistown

American Prairie Reserve 90

Crystal Cascades 91

Libby

Kootenai Falls 92

Livingston

Paradise Valley 93

Lola

Lolo Trail 94

Missoula

Bob Marshall Wilderness.. 95

Caras Park 96

Clark Fork Riverfront Trail... 97

Lolo National Forest 98

Mission Valley-Mission Mountain Wilderness 99

Missoula Art Museum... 100

Missoula Downtown and Hip Strip.............................. 101

Mount Sentinel.. 102

National Bison Range 103

Rattlesnake National Recreation Area......................... 104

Rocky Mountain Elk Foundation Visitor Center 106

St. Francis Xavier Church.. 107

The Historical Museum at Fort Missoula 108

The Historic Wilma Theatre 110

Pryor

Pryor Mountains.. 111

Red Lodge

Beartooth Highway 112

Granite Peak.. 113

Siyeh Bend

Grinnell Glacier 114

Ulm

First Peoples Buffalo Jump State Park......................... 115

West Glacier

Avalanche Lake 116

Going-to-the-Sun Road.. 117

Upper Two Medicine Lake 118

Waterton-Glacier International Peace Park 119

Whitefish

Lake McDonald 120

Stumptown Ice Den.. 121

Whitefish Depot... 122

Whitefish Lake... 123

Whitehall

Lewis and Clark Caverns State Park........................... 124

White Sulphur Springs

Castle Ghost Town... 125

Smith River 126

Proper Planning... 127

How to Use This Book

Welcome to your very own adventure guide to exploring the many wonders of the state of Montana. Not only does this book present the most wonderful places to visit and sights to see in the vast state, but it provides GPS coordinates for Google Maps to make exploring that much easier.

Adventure Guide
Sorted by region, this guide offers over 100 amazing wonders of Montana for you to see and explore. They can be visited in any order and this book will help you keep track of where you've been and where to look forward to going next. Each section describes the area or place, what to look for, how to get there, and what you may need to bring along.

GPS Coordinates
As you can imagine, not all of the locations in this book have a physical address. Fortunately, some of the wonders we list are located either within a National Park or Reserve, or near a city, town, or place of business. For those that are not associated with a specific location, it is easiest to map it using GPS coordinates.

Luckily, Google has a system of codes that converts the coordinates into pin-drop locations that Google Maps can interpret and navigate.

Each adventure in this guide includes GPS coordinates along with a physical address whenever it is available.

It is important to be prepared for poor cell signals. It is recommended that you route your location and make sure that the directions are accessible offline. Depending on your device and the distance of some locations, you may need to travel with a backup battery source.

About Montana

Montana was proclaimed the 41st state in the Union on November 8, 1889. The name Montana has roots in the Spanish word *montaña*, meaning "mountain" or "mountainous country." Montana belongs to a group of the eight states that encompass the Rocky Mountains and are called the "Mountain States." The other seven states are Arizona, Colorado, Idaho, Nevada, New Mexico, Utah, and Wyoming.

Although Montana doesn't have an official nickname, it has acquired several unofficial ones, including "Big Sky Country," "Land of the Singing Mountains," and "the Last Best Place." Montana also earned the nickname "the Treasure State" because of its abundance of gold, silver, copper, lead, zinc, coal, and oil, particularly around the capital city of Helena. "Big Sky Country" refers to the openness of the sky and its vastness because the state is sparsely populated and there aren't many tall buildings.

Montana has an incredible variety of wildlife compared to other U.S. states. Expect to see bison, mountain goats, and grizzly bears, Montana's state animal. Adventurers should be aware that grizzly bear sightings and encounters occur frequently around the state, and you should be cautious about them, along with other dangerous animals such as mountain lions and moose.

Glacier National Park and part of Yellowstone National Park are located in Montana. There are also several national recreation areas, monuments, and historical sites.

Montana is the fourth-largest state in the United States by area at 147,040 square miles, and it is the seventh least populated. The economy of Montana is based primarily on agriculture, especially cattle ranching and growing grain.

Landscape and Climate

Within the vast state of Montana are mountains, canyons, valleys, forests, plains, badlands, and caverns. The topography of Montana is roughly defined by the Continental Divide of the Americas, which splits the state into distinct western and eastern regions.

The western half of Montana is full of mountains and valleys, while the eastern half of the state is characterized by mostly badlands and prairies with some isolated island ranges. The 77 named ranges in Montana are part of the Rocky Mountains. Also belonging to the northern Great Plains, about 60 percent of Montana is prairie.

The climate of Montana varies considerably due to the size of the state and variations in altitude, geography, and topography. Elevation ranges from under 2,000 feet to nearly 13,000 feet above sea level. The state is home to many glacier formations in the western mountain ranges, about 62 of which are of significant size and named.

The western half of the state has a modified northern Pacific Coast climate, which means mild winters, cool summers, and low wind speeds. Daytime temperatures average about 28°F in January and about 85°F in July. Eastern Montana experiences a semi-arid, continental climate with warm summers and cold winters.

The coldest temperatures recorded for the lower 48 states occurred in Montana. Summer nights are generally cool and pleasant across the state, and the winter brings an abundance of snow, especially to the mountainous areas. The humidity remains relatively low all year.

The Garden of One Thousand Buddhas

If you're looking for a place that will provide you with a quiet meditative experience, the Garden of One Thousand Buddhas is a must-see attraction. Located on a Native American reservation in Arlee, this garden was created in 2000 as an international center for peace. The 750-foot circular monument features 1,000 Buddha statues on 10 acres of land.

The monument is arranged in the wheel of dharma formation, representing the Noble Eightfold Path, which symbolizes the eternal cycle of life, death, and rebirth. A central shrine located at the intersection of eight symmetrical spokes features a 24-foot statue of Yum Chenmo, the Great Mother. The garden offers a quiet place for reflection and contemplation.

Best Time to Visit: The best time to visit the Garden of One Thousand Buddhas is during the summer when the weather is warmer.

Pass/Permit/Fees: There is no fee to visit.

Closest City or Town: Arlee

Physical Address: 34574 White Coyote Road, Arlee, MT 59821

GPS Coordinates: 47.1926° N, 114.0897° W

Did You Know? The Garden of One Thousand Buddhas represents the 1,000 Buddhas that followers believe will be born during the religious age.

Apikuni Falls

The hike to Apikuni Falls is only 1.8 miles out and back, but it's steep. The 100-foot waterfall tucked beneath the rocky cliffs is well worth the effort. Surrounded by mountain peaks, meadows, and forestry, it is a scenic route to a beautiful destination.

The trail to the falls begins at the Poia Lake Trailhead, which is 2.8 miles west of the Many Glacier entrance to Glacier National Park. You can reach the falls from the top for a bird's-eye view and continue to hike to the base of the falls.

Best Time to Visit: The best time to visit Apikuni Falls is between June and October.

Pass/Permit/Fees: The summer rate is $35 per vehicle, and the winter rate is $25 per vehicle.

Closest City or Town: Babb

Physical Address: Glacier National Park, 64 Grinnell Drive, West Glacier, MT 59936

GPS Coordinates: 48.8141° N, 113.6426° W

Did You Know? In the Blackfoot language, *Apikuni* can be translated as "Far-Off White Robe," "Spotted Robe," or "Far-Away Robe."

Bowman Lake

Bowman Lake is in the northwestern portion of Glacier National Park. It's a peaceful lake with hiking and recreational opportunities such as fishing, canoeing, and kayaking. Camping is available as well, with a front-country campsite at the head of the lake and a backcountry one at the base. No motorboats are allowed, so it is truly quiet and serene. Traveling to the lake is an adventure in itself and requires traveling a pretty rough road, so good tires and a high-clearance vehicle are warranted. Campers and RVs cannot make the trip.

Numerous hiking opportunities are available, from day-hiking options to multi-day backpacking trips. Many of the hikes start at the Bowman Campground, including the Bowman Lake Trail, which goes 13 miles into deep, secluded forestry for 26 miles round trip.

Best Time to Visit: The best time to visit Bowman Lake is during the summer

Pass/Permit/Fees: The summer rate is $35 per vehicle, and the winter rate is $25 per vehicle.

Closest City or Town: Babb

Physical Address: Head Bowman Lake Campground, West Glacier, MT 59936

GPS Coordinates: 48.9093° N, 114.2017° W

Did You Know? Bowman Lake offers more solitude than other areas of Glacier National Park and has less than 2 million visitors per year.

Cracker Lake Trail

Cracker Lake Trail is a popular 12-mile-long out-and-back trail. The activities available on the trail include hiking, backpacking, camping, walking, and even horseback riding, as horses are allowed to use this trail.

It is a long hike, but it's worth it because it's one of the most beautiful hikes in Glacier. There's something for everyone to enjoy on this trail, and you have the option to travel an extra mile down to the shore of the lake itself for another stunning view.

Best Time to Visit: The best time to visit Cracker Lake Trail is between May and October.

Pass/Permit/Fees: The summer rate is $35 per vehicle, and the winter rate is $25 per vehicle.

Closest City or Town: Babb

Physical Address: Many Glacier Hotel, 1147 Route 3, Browning, MT 59417

GPS Coordinates: 48.7422° N, 113.6436° W

Did You Know? About 6 miles into the hike, on a sunny day, the lake is a bright, beautiful turquoise that is a sight to behold.

Hidden Falls

Beginning near the shoreline of Swiftcurrent Lake at the south end of the Many Glacier Hotel, you can hike around the lake or shave 5 miles off your round trip by taking two shuttle boats across Swiftcurrent Lake and then Lake Josephine. It is a 1.2-mile hike round trip with the boat ride or a 5.2-mile round trip without.

From the second boat landing, proceed to the right along the trail toward Hidden Falls. Travel through a quiet forest and, less than a mile from the boat dock, you'll reach a suspension footbridge. After crossing the bridge, you'll come upon the waterfall.

Best Time to Visit: The best time to visit Hidden Falls is between June and October.

Pass/Permit/Fees: Round-trip boat fees are $18 for adults and $10 for children (ages 2–11). One-way fees are $10 for adults and $8 for children.

Closest City or Town: Babb

Physical Address: Many Glacier Hotel, 1147 Route 3, Browning, MT 59417

GPS Coordinates: 48.7237° N, 113.7495° W

Did You Know? Hidden Falls gets its name from the fact that the falls are not visible from a distance because they are tucked in a deep gorge created by Cataract Creek.

Iceberg Lake

Located in Glacier National Park, the beautiful alpine Iceberg Lake is surrounded by the cliffs of Mount Wilbur, Iceberg Peak, and the Continental Divide, all soaring a few thousand feet higher than the lake. The moderate-rated trail to Iceberg Lake is 9.3 miles out and back and passes through open terrain full of panoramic views of the surrounding mountains, an alpine meadow filled with wildflowers, and brief forested spots.

The trail ends at the emerald-green lake, where many icebergs can be seen floating. The trail is also known for bear sightings, so you may want to bring some bear spray and travel in groups.

Best Time to Visit: The best time to visit Iceberg Lake is between June and October.

Pass/Permit/Fees: Summer rates are $35 per vehicle, $20 per motorcycle, and $20 per individual. Winter rates are $25 per vehicle, $20 per motorcycle, and $15 per individual.

Closest City or Town: Babb

Physical Address: Glacier National Park, 64 Grinnell Drive, West Glacier, MT 59936

GPS Coordinates: 48.8126° N, 113.7480° W

Did You Know? Icebergs float on the lake all year long, even in the summer months. The lake's altitude of over 6,000 feet and shade from over 3,000 feet of mountains and cliffs keep the water very cool.

Lake Josephine

Glacier National Park is home to many beautiful lakes featuring outstanding views. Lake Josephine is a backcountry lake accessible only by hiking or boat. From the Grinnell Glacier Trailhead, it's a 3.4-mile round-trip hike to the lake. You can also take a shortcut by riding a charter boat across the lake, which makes it a 0.2-mile hike.

Lake Josephine and Swiftcurrent Lake are immediately beside each other and connected by a small stream, so when you start hiking, you'll actually go alongside the latter first. The Lake Josephine Trail starts at the upper Swiftcurrent boat dock, runs west, and continues north along the shore of the lake.

Best Time to Visit: The best time to visit Lake Josephine is during the summer.

Pass/Permit/Fees: The summer rate is $35 per vehicle, and the winter rate is $25 per vehicle.

Closest City or Town: Babb

Physical Address: Grinnell Glacier Trailhead, 0 Route 3, Browning, MT 59417

GPS Coordinates: 48.7971° N, 113.6684° W

Did You Know? Although you cannot drive straight to it, Lake Josephine is one of the easiest backcountry lakes to access in Glacier National Park.

Saint Mary Falls

Saint Mary Falls is around 35 feet high. A footbridge offers a great view, and hikers can scramble to get even closer views of the falls. It is a 1.6-mile round trip to Saint Mary Falls, but this destination is easily a two for one because Virginia Falls is a short distance away off a short spur trail, making for a 3.6-mile round trip.

Near the beginning of the trail, you can enjoy beautiful views of 8,064-foot Dusty Star Mountain directly in front of you, 8,922-foot Almost-a-Dog Mountain and 9,541-foot Little Chief Mountain toward the south, and Fusillade, Reynolds, and Heavy Runner mountains to the east.

Best Time to Visit: The best time to visit Saint Mary Falls is during the spring, summer, or fall.

Pass/Permit/Fees: The summer rate is $35 per vehicle, and the winter rate is $25 per vehicle.

Closest City or Town: Babb

Physical Address: Saint Mary Falls Parking Lot, 0 Route 3, Babb, MT 59411

GPS Coordinates: 48.667877° N, 113.615326° W

Did You Know? The water of the falls is turquoise blue because of bits of rock and sediment known as "glacial flour."

Siyeh Pass Trail

Siyeh Pass Trail is another long one, about 10 miles point to point. In addition to featuring a lake, the trail is popular for backpacking, hiking, and day trips to observe nature. This trail offers hikers a safer and more gradual climb up to the pass than the trail beginning at Piegan Pass Trailhead, which adds more distance and quite a bit more climbing to your route.

Unfortunately, because the trail is point to point, visitors need multiple vehicles. Otherwise, they have to take the shuttle because the trail does not loop back around to where it began.

Best Time to Visit: The best time to visit Siyeh Pass Trail is between March and October.

Pass/Permit/Fees: There is no fee for the trail, but the park itself charges by the vehicle.

Closest City or Town: Babb

Physical Address: Siyeh Pass Trailhead, Glacier Route 1 Road/Going-to-the-Sun Road, Browning, MT 59417

GPS Coordinates: 48.6788° N, 113.7328° W

Did You Know? About a third of the way along the trail lies Preston Park, a glacier-carved valley that's famous and popular for its scenic meadows and bounty of wildflowers. This stop is an excellent destination on its own and a good place to visit even in the winter months.

Stoney Indian Pass

The Stoney Indian Pass, named for the tribe that used the trail of the same name, Stoney Indian Trail, was used to reach Belly River Valley to hunt and fish. The trail follows the Cosley Lake shore to the campsite, where open fires are not permitted. The next campsite along the trail, however, does have grates set up and allows visitors to have open fires in the area.

The lower Glenns Lake campsite is a good stopping point before continuing on the main trail, where visitors will eventually find a larger campsite just before the trail begins to get steeper and more difficult. Hikers are rewarded with beautiful views and a variety of flora before the quick, steep descent down the junction using Watertown Valley Trail.

Best Time to Visit: The best time to visit Stoney Indian Pass is in the summer or fall.

Pass/Permit/Fees: There is no fee to visit.

Closest City or Town: Babb

Physical Address: Glacier National Park, 64 Grinnell Drive, West Glacier, MT 59936

GPS Coordinates: 48.8834° N, 113.8643° W

Did You Know? While bears do frequent the area, the dense tree line obscures them, and visitors, from view, keeping risks to a minimum.

Swiftcurrent Lake

Surrounded by mountains and forests, the Many Glacier is one of the most scenic areas of Glacier National Park. Grinnell Glacier is among the glaciers and snowfields that provide water and replenish the lake. Several mountains are visible to the west. Meandering through trees near the shoreline, the loop around Swiftcurrent Lake is one of many trails full of fantastic views.

The loop trail begins at the Many Glacier Hotel and heads south along the shoreline. It is an easy hike around the lake and, if you keep your eyes on the hillsides to the north, you will likely spot wildlife such as bears, bighorn sheep, and mountain goats.

Best Time to Visit: The best time to visit Swiftcurrent Lake is during the summer.

Pass/Permit/Fees: The summer rate is $35 per vehicle, and the winter rate is $25 per vehicle.

Closest City or Town: Babb

Physical Address: Many Glacier Hotel, 1147 Route 3, Browning, MT 59417

GPS Coordinates: 48.7953° N, 113.6574° W

Did You Know? The mountains immediately west of Swiftcurrent Lake rise 3,000 feet above the lake.

Bigfork Art & Cultural Center

With the goal of providing the Bigfork community with a place to gather and celebrate the arts, the Bigfork Art & Cultural Center was conceived in 1977. A group of forward-thinking volunteers raised funds to purchase and renovate a gas station to become its location. Since its establishment, the center has provided a place for Montana artists to display their work and discover new trends and ideas in culture and art.

It also provides creative and educational opportunities for the community at large and for visitors. The Bigfork Art & Cultural Center Museum in the upper gallery features the Bigfork History Project. This interactive exhibit and historical collection educates visitors about local history. The lower gallery features various exhibits throughout the year and is home to Art, etc., a gift shop that sells unique items from local artists, authors, and artisans.

Best Time to Visit: The center is open Tuesday through Saturday from 11:00 a.m. to 5:00 p.m.

Pass/Permit/Fees: There is no fee to visit.

Closest City or Town: Bigfork

Physical Address: 525 Electric Avenue, Bigfork, MT 59911

GPS Coordinates: 48.0631° N, 114.0729° W

Did You Know? Various workshops are open to the public, including seasonal craft sessions.

18

White Cliffs

One of Montana's most beloved scenic wonders is the White Cliffs near the Missouri River. This 46-mile stretch of the river is great for hiking, floating, fishing, and sightseeing. Part of the Upper Missouri River Breaks National Monument, it has geological, biological, and historical significance.

Many visitors choose to travel by water through the area due to its limited road accessibility. From the river, you can view the prairies, plains, and fascinating sandstone rock formations. The classic Missouri float trip is a 4-day, 3-night float through the White Cliffs that launches at Coal Banks Landing and camps at Eagle Creek, Hole in the Wall, and Slaughter River, then takes out at Judith Landing.

Best Time to Visit: The best time to visit the White Cliffs is during the summer.

Pass/Permit/Fees: There is no fee to visit unless you would like a guided tour.

Closest City or Town: Big Sandy

Physical Address: Upper Missouri River Breaks National Monument, 920 NE Main Street, Lewistown, MT 59457

GPS Coordinates: 48.0463° N, 110.2301° W

Did You Know? The White Cliffs are a High Potential Historic Site on the Lewis and Clark National Historic Trail.

Big Sky Resort & Bridger Bowl Ski Area

Known as a premier skiing destination, Big Sky Resort & Bridger Bowl Ski Area is also an excellent place to visit even when there isn't snow on the ground. Located between West Yellowstone and Bozeman, the resort offers breathtaking scenery, sharing many of the same spectacular views as Yellowstone National Park.

In the winter, guests can enjoy Nordic skiing, snowshoe tours, an adventure zipline, a nature zipline, and a hike through the Enchanted Forest. In the summer, they can participate in mountain biking, golfing, scenic lift rides, guided hikes, zipline tours, and the Lone Peak Expedition, which takes visitors to Montana's highest scenic overlook by tram, making it a great adventure for people of any age or fitness level. There are 5,850 skiable acres and 39 ski lifts climbing 4,350 vertical feet inside the Big Sky Resort.

Best Time to Visit: Visit in the winter to take advantage of the numerous snow sports.

Pass/Permit/Fees: Costs depend on the activity you choose and the season you visit. Check the website for pricing.

Closest City or Town: Big Sky

Physical Address: 50 Big Sky Resort Road, Big Sky, MT 59716

GPS Coordinates: 45.2864° N, 111.4015° W

Did You Know? Big Sky Resort has been open since 1973 and has grown steadily in the nearly 50 intervening years, more than tripling the available ski area.

Ousel Falls Park

Ousel Falls Park is home to a small but popular trail of the same name. It's a 1.6-mile out-and-back trail that is friendly to hikers of all levels. One of the attractive elements of this trail is that it allows dogs; many trails in the area do not.

The main activities on the Ousel Falls Park Trail are hiking and walking one's dog, but day trips for sightseeing and nature observation are also great opportunities at this somewhat busy, yet peaceful location. There are views of some intermediate cascades and intriguing cliffs. The trail offers multiple paths, one of which leads to a small picnic area, complete with a table, near the falls.

Best Time to Visit: The best time to visit Ousel Falls Park is during the summer or fall.

Pass/Permit/Fees: There is no fee to visit.

Closest City or Town: Big Sky

Physical Address: Ousel Falls Park, Ousel Falls Road, Gallatin Gateway, MT 59730

GPS Coordinates: 45.2441° N, 111.3326° W

Did You Know? Ousel Falls is named after the ouzel bird, or water ouzel, which is also known as the American dipper. Ousels hunt for water insects and small fish by diving into the water.

Alberta Bair Theatre

For over 80 years, the Alberta Bair Theatre has been a mainstay in Billings. Originally named the Fox Theatre, opening night was on November 13, 1931, and the event was heralded with a parade and street dance. The first motion picture to show at the theater was *Merely Mary Ann*. The theater was home to the Billings Community Concerts Organization and the Billings Symphony Orchestra & Chorale.

When new owners wanted to completely renovate the historic theater in 1978, the Fox Committee protested by raising funds to buy back the building and restore it to its original Art Deco glory. The theater sits on what used to be the homestead of Charles M. Bair. In 1987, the theater was renamed in honor of Mrs. Bair.

Best Time to Visit: The best time to visit the Alberta Bair Theatre is when there is a show on stage that you want to see. Check the website for show dates and times.

Pass/Permit/Fees: Prices vary with show and seat selection.

Closest City or Town: Billings

Physical Address: 2801 3rd Avenue North, Billings, MT 59103

GPS Coordinates: 45.78434° N, 108.50777° W

Did You Know? The Alberta Bair Theatre has hosted many famous singers, musicians, and actors, including Dizzy Gillespie, Judy Collins, and Ray Charles.

Billings Studio Theatre

The Billings Studio Theatre is home to a vibrant volunteer-based community theater group that has performed in the area for more than 60 years. Originally, the Billings Studio Theatre was a Sunday evening play-reading group that met in the homes of early members. Eventually, it grew into a theater group that performed in donated spaces at Eastern Montana College and the YWCA. The group then began to perform on radio and stage and conducted workshops in various facets of theater and the dramatic arts.

In 1963, the group found what they thought would be a permanent home in a remodeled church in downtown Billings, but the church was condemned and torn down 5 years later. Funds were raised for a new building that opened in November 1971 and continues to serve the Billings Studio Theatre to this day.

Best Time to Visit: The best time to visit the Billings Studio Theatre is when a show is playing that you want to see. Check the website for show dates and times.

Pass/Permit/Fees: The fee depends on the show and seat selection.

Closest City or Town: Billings

Physical Address: 1500 Rimrock Road, Billings, MT 59102

GPS Coordinates: 45.7993° N, 108.5539° W

Did You Know? The first play that the Billings Studio Theatre presented in 1953 was *There's Always Juliet*.

Centennial Park

Centennial Park is the newest addition to Billings, having opened in fall 2020. The first community park built in the city since the early 1980s, it has two large multi-purpose open spaces, several baseball fields, and a 6-acre fenced-off dog park that opened in June 2021.

The park was approved in July 2019 and constructed in two phases. The first phase included grading and irrigation, and the second phase included the construction of the dog park. Approximately $80,000 in funds was raised by the Friends of Billings Dog Parks to install the fence, shade structures, and informational signage. In addition to a few other amenities, the park has a paved sidewalk, a parking lot, and a lot of grass.

Best Time to Visit: The best time to visit Centennial Park is during the spring, summer, or fall when the weather is warm.

Pass/Permit/Fees: There is no fee to visit.

Closest City or Town: Billings

Physical Address: 32nd Street West and St. Johns Avenue, Billings, MT 59101

GPS Coordinates: 45.7724° N, 108.5982° W

Did You Know? The Centennial Dog Park at Centennial Park was the first dog park in Billings.

DanWalt Gardens

Once part of a 10-acre vegetable farm, DanWalt Gardens is now the top-rated garden in the entire state. It boasts 1.5 acres of flowering annuals, perennials, trees, and shrubs. Water features and statuaries make it a popular location for weddings, corporate events, and private parties.

No matter what season it is, there are always flower displays to see, along with an outdoor bar, pavilion, and service kitchen. A ceremony pergola and a bridal room are also available for weddings. The gardens include a parterre, a rose garden, a Japanese garden, and a ceremony garden.

Best Time to Visit: The gardens are open from May 1 to October 15, 9:00 a.m. to 6:00 p.m., so it depends on the type of flowers you want to see. Tulips bloom in April, roses in June, and dahlias in October. Check the website to see when your favorite flower will appear.

Pass/Permit/Fees: Adult admission is $7.50 per person. Children ages 12 and under are free.

Closest City or Town: Billings

Physical Address: 720 Washington Street, Billings, MT 59101

GPS Coordinates: 45.7559° N, 108.5106° W

Did You Know? The DanWalt Gardens are named for Dan Jellison and Walt Williams, who lived on a 1-acre parcel of the Jellison/Jost property and converted their back yard into garden areas.

Dehler Park

This multi-use stadium in Billings is used mainly for baseball practice and games. It is the home of the Billings Mustangs, a professional baseball team in the independent Pioneer League. The Billings American Legion team and the Montana State University of Billings Yellowjackets also play their home games at Dehler Park.

The park has been open since June 2008, when it replaced Cobb Field, a stadium that dated back to the 1930s. The capacity of Dehler Park is 3,071 people seated and 6,000 with standing room. Part of Cobb Field still exists within the new stadium because some of the bench seating in right field was transferred from the old stadium to the new one to preserve history.

Best Time to Visit: The best time to visit Dehler Park is during baseball season between April and October.

Pass/Permit/Fees: The fee to visit Dehler Park depends on game and seat selection.

Closest City or Town: Billings

Physical Address: 2611 9th Avenue North, Billings, MT 59101

GPS Coordinates: 45.7913° N, 108.5111° W

Did You Know? Dehler Park is named for Billy Joe Dehler, father of Billings businessman Jon Dehler, who purchased the naming rights to the park in 2007 to honor his father.

Four Dances Recreation Area

This 765-acre undeveloped open space is a designated special recreation area located on a plateau just 2 miles east of downtown Billings. Cliffs bordering the plateau drop up to 500 feet to the Yellowstone River. The open land is used for environmental education, wildlife watching, hiking, and nature photography.

To protect its delicate ecosystem, Four Dances Recreation Area is closed to motorized vehicles, horses, fireworks, rock climbing, hang gliding, hunting, paintball activities, and off-leash pets. A 3-mile hiking loop through the area is rated as moderate for its elevation changes. The views of Billings from the top of the sandstone cliffs are breathtaking, and the hike to the river is full of other scenic stops that photographers won't be able to skip.

Best Time to Visit: The best time to visit Four Dances Recreation Center is spring, summer, or fall when the weather is warmer.

Pass/Permit/Fees: There is no fee to visit.

Closest City or Town: Billings

Physical Address: 5001 Southgate Drive, Billings, MT 59101

GPS Coordinates: 45.7779° N, 108.4731° W

Did You Know? Be sure to look for the historic *Yegen Bros* writing on the cliffs, which was an early 1900s advertisement for Peter Yegen's clothing and shoe store.

Lake Elmo State Park

The 64-acre Elmo State Park is a popular place for locals to fish, swim, paddleboard, picnic, hike, and birdwatch. The reservoir is a favorite of anglers who come to fish for rainbow trout, smallmouth bass, largemouth bass, cutthroat trout, and channel catfish, among others.

A playground and two shelters allow for large gatherings, and a 200-square-foot dog park is open for dogs that are at least four months old. The water area and off-leash freedom make this amenity fun for dogs and their owners. In the winter, the reservoir is open for ice fishing and ice skating when it freezes over.

Best Time to Visit: The best time to visit Lake Elmo State Park is during the summer for fishing, swimming, and paddle boarding or in the winter for ice fishing and ice skating.

Pass/Permit/Fees: Montana residents pay a $9 state park fee when they register their vehicles each year. Nonresidents have to pay a fee of $8 per vehicle, and the walk-in fee is $4 per person.

Closest City or Town: Billings

Physical Address: 2300 Lake Elmo Drive, Billings, MT 59105

GPS Coordinates: 45.8390° N, 108.4770° W

Did You Know? In September 2021, Lake Elmo was partially drained to kill an invasive species of Asian clams.

MetraPark

This 189-acre multi-use complex in Billings is the home of the Montana State Fair, livestock and equestrian shows, trade events, conventions, and numerous other entertainment and sporting activities.

Among events that have been held at MetraPark are the No Limits Monster Truck show, a Dierks Bentley concert, a Jeff Dunham performance, the All-American Indian Shootout competition, the Super A Divisional Basketball tournament, the Sports Connection Gun Show, the Festival of Trees, the Great Rockies Sportshow, the Building & Remodeling Expo, and others.

Best Time to Visit: The best time to visit the MetraPark is when there is an event there that you want to attend. See the website for event dates and times.

Pass/Permit/Fees: Fees vary depending on the event.

Closest City or Town: Billings

Physical Address: 308 6th Avenue North, Billings, MT 59101

GPS Coordinates: 45.8010° N, 108.4773° W

Did You Know? The actual name of MetraPark is First Interstate Arena, but it is locally known as the Metra.

Montana Audubon Conservation Education Center

The center was founded in 1976 to promote the statewide conservation of Montana's native birds, wildlife, and natural ecosystems. The Montana Audubon's mission is to create an environment that allows all of the state's native bird species to have healthy and sustainable populations that are supported by long-term habitat security.

On the center's property, five trails take visitors past two ponds, a marsh, and Prior Hill. These trails range in length from 0.3 miles to 0.6 miles.

Best Time to Visit: The grounds of the Montana Audubon Conservation Education Center are open from dawn until dusk. The best time to visit is in the summer when the weather is warmer.

Pass/Permit/Fees: There is no fee to visit.

Closest City or Town: Billings

Physical Address: 7026 S. Billings Boulevard, Billings, MT 59191

GPS Coordinates: 45.7435° N, 108.5393° W

Did You Know? The Montana Audubon Conservation Education Center offers various year-round programs including Nature Nuts for children ages 1 to 4 and Weekend Wonders Family Programs for visitors of all ages.

Moss Mansion Museum

Constructed in 1903 by entrepreneur Preston Boyd Moss, the Moss Mansion was designed by renowned New York architect Henry Janeway Hardenbergh, who also designed the original Waldorf Astoria and Plaza hotels. The Moss Mansion is a showcase of superior craftsmanship, exquisite décor, and inspirational architecture.

The mansion has been featured in movies like *Return to Lonesome Dove* and *Son of the Morning Star*. Melville Moss, one of Preston Boyd Moss's five children, lived in the house until the mid-1980s, and all original fixtures remain in the home today. Many of the mansion's amenities were unheard of in the early 20th century, including heated indoor plumbing, an electric bell system for calling servants, and a rotary telephone.

Best Time to Visit: The Moss Mansion Museum is open Wednesday through Monday from 12:00 p.m. to 3:00 p.m.

Pass/Permit/Fees: Admission is $15 for adults and $12 for seniors or students ages 6 to 18. Children ages 5 and under are free.

Closest City or Town: Billings

Physical Address: 914 Division Street, Billings, MT 59101

GPS Coordinates: 45.7802° N, 108.5161° W

Did You Know? The Moss Mansion Museum hosts a walking tour of the historic neighborhood around the house.

Pictograph Cave State Park

Previously home to generations of prehistoric hunters, Pictograph Cave State Park is now home to many artifacts and rock paintings, or pictographs. Images of animals, warriors, and rifles tell stories from hundreds to thousands of years ago in this National Historic Landmark.

Full of history that needs to be preserved, the caves can be viewed but not entered by hikers. There are three main caves to view: Pictograph, Middle, and Ghost Cave. A 0.75-mile loop trail brings you to the caves, passing interpretive displays along the route. Visitors are advised to bring binoculars to best view the rock art inside the caves.

Best Time to Visit: The best time to visit Pictograph Cave State Park is during the summer.

Pass/Permit/Fees: The day-use entry fee is $8 for vehicles and $4 for walk-ins, bicycles, or bus passengers. Montana residents who pay the $9 state park fee with their vehicle registration don't have to pay daily entrance fees.

Closest City or Town: Billings

Physical Address: 3401 Coburn Road, Billings, MT 59101

GPS Coordinates: 45.7374° N, 108.4315° W

Did You Know? The oldest rock art in the cave is estimated to be over 2,000 years old, and the most recent additions are between 200 and 500 years old.

Reef Indoor Water Park

As the largest indoor water park in Montana, Reef Indoor Water Park is a popular destination during all seasons of the year. Visitors are treated to the 3-story Barracuda Blaster and Tropical Twister water slides, a 55,000-gallon wave pool, and a water basketball area. There's also an interactive playhouse for younger guests, which includes slides, squirt guns, a 250-gallon dumping bucket, tunnels, and mini-tubes.

It's an excellent place for a group gathering, especially with all the tables on the enclosed patio and surrounding the water park. When you get hungry, the Shark Shack, a snack bar located inside the water park, has you covered.

Best Time to Visit: The Reef Indoor Water Park is currently open only on Saturday and Sunday. Check the website for updated hours.

Pass/Permit/Fees: Admission is $18 for anyone over 48 inches tall and $16 for everyone else. Discounts are available for hotel guests.

Closest City or Town: Billings

Physical Address: 1801 Majestic Lane, Billings, MT 59102

GPS Coordinates: 45.7354° N, 108.6035° W

Did You Know? The Reef Indoor Water Park also features a 20-person hot tub, arcade games, a gift shop, and locker rooms with a public showering area.

Riverfront Park

Located along the Yellowstone River, Riverfront Park is just south of downtown Billings. This park is an ideal way to escape from the city without actually leaving it. You can dip your toes in the river, enjoy a picnic lunch among the trees, or simply relax and watch the varied wildlife that calls the park home. Lake Josephine is in the park, along with 7 miles of trails for hiking, biking, and rollerblading.

Other amenities at Riverfront Park include volleyball courts, barbecue grills, picnic sites, and public toilets. Fishing is allowed in Lake Josephine, where you can catch bass, channel catfish, crappies, sunfish, and tiger muskies. It's an excellent lake for beginning anglers because it is easily accessible from the park.

Best Time to Visit: The best time to visit Riverfront Park is during the spring and summer when the weather is warmer.

Pass/Permit/Fees: There is no fee to visit.

Closest City or Town: Billings

Physical Address:
7277–7337 State Secondary Highway 416, Billings, MT 59101

GPS Coordinates: 45.7420° N, 108.5338° W

Did You Know? Cochran Pond in Riverfront Park is often used for fishing and dog swimming.

The Rimrocks

Also referred to as "the Rims," the Rimrocks are an outcrop of sandstone formations that are located near Billings. About 80 million years ago, the Billings area was the shore of the Western Interior Seaway, which stretched from the Gulf of Mexico to the Arctic North. Sand and sediment from this sea were deposited on the shore and, over time, a deep layer of sand built up. Over millions of years, the sand became compressed into the Rimrocks.

Several parks are located on the Rimrocks, including Swords Park, the Four Dances Natural Area, and Zimmerman Park. Hiking is an extremely popular activity in and around the Rimrocks, with Yellowstone Kelly's gravesite and the Angel statue that overlooks Rocky Mountain College as two favorite destinations. From the top of the Rimrocks, visitors are treated to a spectacular view of the Billings Metro Area.

Best Time to Visit: The best time to visit the Rimrocks is in the summer when the weather is warm and dry.

Pass/Permit/Fees: There is no fee to visit.

Closest City or Town: Billings

Physical Address: Billings Visitor Center, 815 S. 27th Street, Billings, MT 59107

GPS Coordinates: 45.7593° N, 108.5021° W

Did You Know? The Rimrocks were carved by the Yellowstone River.

Western Heritage Center

Established in 1971, the Western Heritage Center got its start as a community center that displayed a private collection of western artifacts. Located in the historic library building, it currently boasts a collection of 40,000 historic photographs and artifacts, along with more than 400 oral histories.

The building itself is a work of art, having been constructed in 1901. It is a shining example of Romanesque sandstone, and it's listed on the National Register of Historic Places. In addition to the museum's collection, there are also rotating interactive exhibits, 12 traveling displays, and several outreach programs and walking tours.

Best Time to Visit: The Western Heritage Center is open Tuesday through Saturday from 10:00 a.m. to 5:00 p.m.

Pass/Permit/Fees: Admission is $5 for adults, $3 for seniors and students, and $1 for children under the age of 12.

Closest City or Town: Billings

Physical Address: 2822 Montana Avenue, Billings, MT 59101

GPS Coordinates: 45.7807° N, 108.5058° W

Did You Know? In 2021, the Western Heritage Center celebrated 50 years of incorporation and introduced virtual exhibits to reach a broader audience.

Yellowstone Art Museum

This museum opened as the Yellowstone Art Center in Billings in 1964 to display contemporary avant-garde artwork instead of the Western art of the time. The Yellowstone Art Museum focuses on modern art that originated in the northern Rockies region. It collects art from every period and emphasizes work from artists in Montana and the American Northwest.

The museum's collection also includes historic and contemporary art that is considered influential for regional audiences and that which serves as an interpretive foundation for art-making processes in the region.

Best Time to Visit: The Yellowstone Art Museum is open Tuesday, Wednesday, Friday, Saturday, and Sunday from 10:00 a.m. to 5:00 p.m. On Thursday and the first Friday of each month, it's open late until 8:00 p.m.

Pass/Permit/Fees: Admission is $15 for adults, $12 for seniors ages 65 and up, and $6 for children ages 6 to 18. Children under the age of 6 are free.

Closest City or Town: Billings

Physical Address: 401 N. 27th Street, Billings, MT 59101

GPS Coordinates: 45.7863° N, 108.5072° W

Did You Know? The museum is housed in the former Yellowstone County Jail.

Yellowstone Cellars & Winery

This local winery prides itself on using only local red and white grapes that are grown in Columbia Valley and Yakima Valley vineyards. Its wines are made from traditional premium vinifera wine grapes that are the foundation of the wines produced in Old World regions like Bordeaux, Rhone, Loire, Burgundy, and Rhine.

The winery has a tasting room, wine cellar, and event area, where visitors can enjoy samples of the winery's premium wines. Guests can also tour the cellar and taste some wines directly from the barrels as they age. Clint Peck, the founder and operator of the winery, undertook this venture after 30 years of running a cattle ranch in central Montana.

Best Time to Visit: The Yellowstone Cellars & Winery is open Monday through Thursday from 1:00 p.m. to 9:00 p.m., from 1:00 p.m. to 11:00 p.m. on Friday and Saturday, and from 1:00 p.m. to 7:00 p.m. on Sunday.

Pass/Permit/Fees: There is no fee to visit, but bring some cash for tastings.

Closest City or Town: Billings

Physical Address: 1335 Holiday Circle, Billings, MT 59101

GPS Coordinates: 45.7468° N, 108.5532° W

Did You Know? All wines produced at Yellowstone Cellars & Winery are available for purchase by the glass, bottle, or case.

Yellowstone County Museum

Yellowstone County Museum was founded in 1953 by the Yellowstone Historical Society, the Parmly Billings Library, the Pioneers of Eastern Montana, the City of Billings, and Yellowstone County. The museum collects, preserves, interprets, and researches the natural history of the Yellowstone Valley of Montana and the Northern Plains.

It offers an impressive number of exhibits and educational programs to help enrich the diverse culture of the community. The Paul McCormick cabin, which was built in 1893 for social gatherings, is the museum's entrance and gift shop. The cabin was moved in 1954 from the original site to its present location to establish the museum.

Best Time to Visit: The Yellowstone County Museum is open Tuesday through Saturday from 10:30 a.m. to 5:30 p.m.

Pass/Permit/Fees: There is no fee to visit.

Closest City or Town: Billings

Physical Address: 1950 Terminal Circle, Billings, MT 59105

GPS Coordinates: 45.8032° N, 108.5378° W

Did You Know? Museum patrons can help support the Yellowstone County Museum by purchasing a Montana Avenue brick for $200. The brick can be engraved with text and graphics and will be permanently placed near the museum's entrance.

ZooMontana

This zoological and botanical garden, arboretum, and educational facility was incorporated as a nonprofit organization in 1984. The only zoological and botanical park within 500 miles of Billings, it features 70 acres of habitat for more than 80 animals belonging to 56 species. Visitors will see grizzly bears, Amur tigers, wolverines, river otters, Canada Lynx, and takins, most of which are rescues.

ZooMontana is one of only a few zoological parks in the country that does not receive funds from public taxes; it operates solely on funds received through memberships, admission, private contributions, and events.

Best Time to Visit: ZooMontana is open daily from 10:00 a.m. to 2:00 p.m., but hours may differ depending on the season.

Pass/Permit/Fees: Admission is $11 for adults, $9 for seniors ages 55 and up, and $8 for children ages 3 to 15. Children ages 2 and under are free.

Closest City or Town: Billings

Physical Address: 2100 S. Shiloh Road, Billings, MT 59106

GPS Coordinates: 45.7329° N, 108.6207° W

Did You Know? More than 15,000 students and 120,000 visitors benefit from ZooMontana's educational programs each year.

American Computer & Robotics Museum

The American Computer & Robotics Museum has been touted as the best museum of its kind. Its exhibits tell the history of the Information Age, going back 4,000 years to the original cuneiform tablets. Founded in 1990, the museum explores topics such as quantum computing, the space race, artificial intelligence, cracking the Enigma code, and much more.

Originally named the American Computer Museum, it was renamed to better reflect its scope. It's believed to be the oldest museum dedicated to computer history still in existence in the U.S. Exhibits include the Apple I personal computer, the NASA Apollo Program, and exhibits related to Enigma codebreaking during World War II.

Best Time to Visit: The American Computer & Robotics Museum is open daily from 10:00 a.m. to 4:00 p.m.

Pass/Permit/Fees: Admission is $7.50 for adults and $4 for seniors ages 65 and older or children ages 10 to 17. Children ages 9 and under are free.

Closest City or Town: Bozeman

Physical Address: 2023 Stadium Drive, Suite 1-A, Bozeman, MT 59715

GPS Coordinates: 45.6601° N, 111.0548° W

Did You Know? The American Computer & Robotics Museum has been rated the #1 Thing to Do in Bozeman and has earned a Certificate of Excellence from TripAdvisor for 6 years in a row.

Bozeman Hot Springs

Bozeman Hot Springs has been a popular destination for relaxation and rejuvenation since the late 1800s. What started as a small pool has grown into a unique experience that combines the therapy of naturally heated water with the gorgeous landscape of wild Montana.

The facility uses a flow-through system to clean the 12 pools and the dry and wet saunas. No chemicals are involved. Visitors can use the full fitness facility before they soak in the hot springs.

Best Time to Visit: The Bozeman Hot Springs is open Monday through Thursday from 5:30 a.m. to 11:00 p.m., Friday from 5:30 a.m. to sundown, Saturday from sundown to 12:00 a.m., and Sunday from 8:00 a.m. to 11:00 p.m.

Pass/Permit/Fees: Adult admission ranges from $17 to $21 depending on the day. Children ages 5 to 13 range from $15 to $17, and children ages 4 and under range from $10 to $12. Holidays are more expensive.

Closest City or Town: Bozeman

Physical Address: 81123 Gallatin Road, Bozeman, MT 59718

GPS Coordinates: 45.6612° N, 111.1874° W

Did You Know? Jeremiah Mathews initially purchased the springs in 1879 and built a bathhouse near the springs.

Bridger Bowl

The nonprofit Bridger Bowl is known as one of the best ski areas in North America. The summit of the mountain is 8,700 feet above sea level, and the terrain offers areas for beginners through experts. Ski and snowboard rentals and snow-sports lessons are available.

The locally owned Bridger Bowl offers affordable skiing and hiking. The 5-mile round trip Bridger Bowl Trail is a difficult trail that steeply ascends to the ridge, where you'll be rewarded with sweeping vistas of Gallatin Mountain and Bridger Canyon.

Best Time to Visit: The best time to visit Bridger Bowl is mid-January to mid-March for skiing or spring for hiking.

Pass/Permit/Fees: Tickets are required for skiing and ski lifts. Daily rates are $69 to $84 for adults, $28 to $43 for children ages 7 to 12, and $44 to $59 for children ages 13 and up. Seasonal passes are available.

Closest City or Town: Bozeman

Physical Address: 15795 Bridger Canyon Road, Bozeman, MT 59715

GPS Coordinates: 45.8174° N, 110.8966° W

Did You Know? Montana has hosted the NCAA Skiing Championships at Bridger Bowl eight times—in 1960, 1983, 1985, 1996, 1998, 2008, 2012, and 2020.

College "M" Hiking Trail

This 1.6-mile hiking loop is an easy-to-moderate trail that starts at the mouth of Bridger Canyon and ends at the giant *M* first created by Montana State University students in 1915. Students still hike to the *M* during homecoming weekend. There are actually two routes that both start at the same trailhead. One is steep and the other is winding.

The steep climb is to the right at the first junction, and the easier route is to the left. It will only take about 30 minutes to hike to the *M* and back unless you linger at the landmark to take in the views of Bozeman. This is probably the most popular trail on the Main Street to the Mountains system.

Best Time to Visit: Avoid the College *M* Hiking Trail during homecoming weekend if you want a more leisurely experience.

Pass/Permit/Fees: There is no fee to visit.

Closest City or Town: Bozeman

Physical Address: Bozeman Information Center, 2000 Commerce Way, Bozeman, MT 59715

GPS Coordinates: 45.7154° N, 110.9734° W

Did You Know? The white rock *M* on the side of the mountain is 250 feet tall and sits about 6,000 feet above the trailhead, which is already 5,000 feet above sea level.

Custer Gallatin National Forest

At more than 3 million acres in area, the Custer Gallatin National Forest offers one of the most ecologically diverse landscapes in Montana. There are three gateways to Yellowstone National Park from the national forest and more than 1 million acres of wilderness that feature mountains, bluffs, and buttes. The Custer Gallatin National Forest is full of grizzly and black bears, so if you are hiking through the area, be sure to carry bear spray and know how to use it.

Camping, picnicking, cycling, fishing, scenic driving, horseback riding, hiking, cross-country skiing, and other recreational opportunities are popular in the forest.

Best Time to Visit: Visit the forest during the spring, summer, and fall when the weather is warmer.

Pass/Permit/Fees: There is no fee to visit except for special events.

Closest City or Town: Bozeman

Physical Address: Bozeman Information Center, 2000 Commerce Way, Bozeman, MT 59715

GPS Coordinates: 45.2442° N, 109.8854° W

Did You Know? Custer Gallatin National Forest is named for Albert Gallatin, who was the U.S. Secretary of the Treasury in the 1800s.

Gallatin History Museum

Located in Bozeman, the Gallatin History Museum offers a unique view of the area's past. Visitors can see jail cells; a hanging gallows; exhibits on the Big Horn Gun, women, music, agriculture, and the jail; a life-size pioneer cabin; and a photo archive of over 20,000 historic images that tell the stories of local places, topics, and families.

Newspapers, maps, yearbooks, oral histories, history books, and family histories are also available and can be reproduced for a small fee. The museum was founded in 1982 as the Pioneer Museum, but the name was changed to the Gallatin History Museum in 2014 to better reflect the museum's collections and mission. The Gallatin Historical Society operates the museum and is also housed in the building.

Best Time to Visit: The Gallatin History Museum is open Tuesday through Saturday from 11:00 a.m. to 4:00 p.m.

Pass/Permit/Fees: Admission is $7.50 for adults and $5 for seniors ages 62 and up. Children under the age of 18 are free.

Closest City or Town: Bozeman

Physical Address: 317 W. Main Street, Bozeman, MT 59715

GPS Coordinates: 45.6805° N, 111.0422° W

Did You Know? The Gallatin History Museum is housed in the city's first jail, which was built in 1911.

Gallatin River

Featuring overhead cliffs, moss-covered boulders, and lodgepole pine forests, the Gallatin River area is full of beauty. The river begins in Gallatin Lake, high in the mountains of the Gallatin Range in Yellowstone National Park, and flows to where it meets the Missouri River. It ranks as one of the finest wade-fishing rivers in Montana.

The Gallatin Riverside Trail is an excellent way to explore part of the river. The trail is 5.5 miles round trip, rated easy, and can be done one way or out and back. You can extend the trip into Gallatin Canyon for even more peaceful nature time.

Best Time to Visit: The best time to visit the Gallatin River is spring, summer, or fall.

Pass/Permit/Fees: There is no fee to visit.

Closest City or Town: Bozeman

Physical Address: Gallatin County Regional Park, 5000 Tschache Lane, Bozeman, MT 59718

GPS Coordinates: 45.7059° N, 111.0885° W

Did You Know? The Gallatin River is one of the best whitewater runs in the Yellowstone-Tatin Area, and it's most challenging section is named the "Mad Mile."

Hyalite Canyon Recreation Area

This is the most popular recreation area in Montana. It is split into three separate campgrounds and has two day-use areas. The campgrounds offer varied experiences, and it is recommended that visitors see each of them at least once.

The first is Langohr Campground, which offers visitors a chance to view wildlife and also has places to fish. Next, there's Hood Creek Campground and finally Chisholm Campground. These areas are the starting points for various trails, both short and long, for hiking and biking.

Best Time to Visit: The best time to visit Hyalite Canyon is during the summer.

Pass/Permit/Fees: There is no fee to visit.

Closest City or Town: Bozeman

Physical Address: Langohr Campground, 6 miles S on Hyalite Canyon Road, Bozeman, MT 59718

GPS Coordinates: 45.5796° N, 111.0791° W

Did You Know? Hyalite Canyon has "no-wake" rules in place, so canoeing and fishing in the summer are safe and fun. The area also has various winter events available, including ice climbing, skiing, and skating.

Little Bighorn Battlefield National Monument

This monument memorializes the Battle of Little Bighorn, which was one of the last efforts of Native Americans to preserve their way of life. On June 25 and 26, 1876, more than 260 soldiers died during the fight between the U.S. Army's 7th Calvary and several thousand Lakota and Cheyenne warriors.

Before the battle, Lakota leaders Crazy Horse and Sitting Bull rejected a plan to move their tribe to reservations, setting the stage for conflict. Visitors can walk in the steps of the fighters at Little Bighorn by driving the tour road from the visitor center through the battlefield.

Best Time to Visit: Visit the Little Bighorn Battlefield National Monument during the spring, summer, or fall.

Pass/Permit/Fees: The fee to visit the Little Bighorn Battlefield National Monument is $10 per private vehicle and $5 for pedestrians.

Closest City or Town: Bozeman

Physical Address: Bozeman Convention and Visitors Bureau, 2000 Commerce Way, Bozeman, MT 59715

GPS Coordinates: 45.5702° N, 107.4324° W

Did You Know? The Battle of the Little Bighorn is also called "Custer's Last Stand" after Lieutenant Colonel George A. Custer, who lost his life during this epic battle.

Montana Grizzly Encounter

At Montana Grizzly Encounter, visitors get up close and personal with four grizzly bears that were rescued by the facility in 2004. Two of these bears, Sheena and Maggi, were born in captivity and have never been in the wild. These bears were rescued from inhumane captive situations. Bella and Max, the two other bears, were born in the wild but were orphaned at a young age in Alaska.

Each year, guests are invited to learn about grizzly bears as they observe them in a natural environment. There are no bars or cages to get in the way of seeing these magnificent creatures. Montana Grizzly Encounter aims to teach people of all ages about grizzly bear conservation.

Best Time to Visit: Montana Grizzly Encounter is open from 10:00 a.m. to at least 4:00 p.m., depending on the season and day. Check the website for exact hours.

Pass/Permit/Fees: Admission is $9 for visitors ages 13 and up, $8 for seniors ages 65 and up, and $7 for children ages 4 to 12.

Closest City or Town: Bozeman

Physical Address: 80 Bozeman Hill Road, Bozeman, MT 59715

GPS Coordinates: 45.6639° N, 110.8340° W

Did You Know? Four other bears have called the Montana Grizzly Encounter home but have passed away due to age or illness. There are memorials to these bears around the facility.

50

Potosi Hot Springs

Offering an ideal mountain-oasis retreat, Potosi Hot Springs are natural mineral hot springs with incredibly pristine waters. Surrounded by stunning canyon views and forests, the springs are located on an 80-acre hideaway. The main pool sits on a moss-dripping granite cliff and offers an incredible canyon view. It is connected by a spring-warmed walking path to a Finnish wood-fired sauna.

Upper Potosi Hot Springs trail is a 1.6-mile out-and-back trail that usually isn't very busy. The trail is fairly easy and appropriate for all skill levels. Available activities include hiking, birdwatching, and picnicking. Dogs are allowed on the trail if they are kept on a leash.

Best Time to Visit: The best time to visit Potosi Hot Springs is between June and September.

Pass/Permit/Fees: There is no fee to visit.

Closest City or Town: Bozeman

Physical Address: Potosi Campground and Picnic Area, 420 Barrett Street, Dillon, MT 59725

GPS Coordinates: 45.5892° N, 111.8998° W

Did You Know? Potosi Hot Springs is currently accessible only to those staying in the cabins on site.

Spotted Bear Ranch

Located in northwest Montana between Glacier National Park and the Bob Marshall Wilderness, Spotted Bear Ranch provides outdoorsmen with the perfect fishing and hunting experience. The ranch is equipped with modern amenities such as Wi-Fi, chef-prepared meals, laundry service, and a bar to help anglers and hunters relax between outings, but the best amenity is the ability to enter into an authentic Montana wilderness by simply stepping outside your cabin.

The scenery is breathtaking no matter what season you visit. You'll get your fill of wild rivers, dense forests, and snowcapped mountain peaks.

Best Time to Visit: The best time for fly fishing in Montana is in May and June. Elk season runs from September through mid-October for archers and mid-October through the end of November for riflemen.

Pass/Permit/Fees: The fee to visit Spotted Bear Ranch depends on your choice of fly fishing or hunting and the time of year you visit.

Closest City or Town: Bozeman

Physical Address: 510 W. Hemlock, Bozeman, MT 59715

GPS Coordinates: 47.9262° N, 113.5306° W

Did You Know? Spotted Bear Ranch offers guided fishing and hunting experiences or more rugged backcountry packages that are customized for each visitor's bucket-list trip.

The Museum of the Rockies

The Museum of the Rockies is a world-class cultural and natural history museum that houses an extensive collection of dinosaur fossils. It is home to the fully mounted *Montana's T. rex* skeleton. The museum also offers rotating natural and cultural history exhibits from around the globe, planetarium shows, educational programs, lectures, fundraising events, and a gift shop.

The museum is a college-level division of Montana State University and an affiliate of the Smithsonian. It is a member of the Association of Science-Technology Centers, the Montana Dinosaur Trail, and the Travel Passport Program.

Best Time to Visit: The Museum of the Rockies is open daily from 9:00 a.m. to 5:00 p.m.

Pass/Permit/Fees: Admission is $16.50 for adults, $10.50 for children ages 5 to 17, $15.50 for seniors ages 65 and up, and free for children under the age of 5. Montana State University students, staff, faculty, and alumni are $12 per person.

Closest City or Town: Bozeman

Physical Address: 600 W. Kagy Boulevard, Bozeman, MT 59717

GPS Coordinates: 45.6593° N, 111.0449° W

Did You Know? The Museum of the Rockies was founded in 1957 and now houses the largest collection of dinosaur fossils in the U.S.

Ringing Rocks

This is one of the most unique geological formations in the world. When lightly tapped with a hammer, the rocks ring like chimes. Geologists believe that the ringing occurs because of the rock composition along with the way the rocks have been joined together through erosion. If a rock is removed from the formation, it does not ring, so the phenomenon is related to how the rocks are arranged together and not because the rocks are different from other similarly composed rocks.

However, despite the effort to establish the scientific reason behind the chiming, no solid explanation has yet been found. There are thousands of rocks in the foundation, each producing a different timbre or pitch.

Best Time to Visit: The best time to visit the Ringing Rocks is during the spring or summer when the weather is more predictable.

Pass/Permit/Fees: There is no fee to visit.

Closest City or Town: Butte

Physical Address: Butte Montana Visitors Center, 1000 George Street, Butte, MT 59701

GPS Coordinates: 45.9453° N, 112.2373° W

Did You Know? In theory, with the range of notes these rocks are capable of producing, the Ringing Rocks of Montana could play the basic ostinato for the "music of the spheres."

The World Museum of Mining

In 1963, the demise of Butte's mining industry was still about 20 years away, but the community realized it needed a museum to document and preserve the history of mining in the area. Butte was home to one of the most productive copper mines in the world, and the museum sought to celebrate this distinction.

Located on an actual mine yard (the Orphan Girl Mine), the museum boasts 50 buildings, thousands of artifacts, and 66 exhibits situated in the mine yard. Plan to spend at least a couple of hours exploring the history of mining in Butte, the U.S., and around the world. As you walk the streets of Hell Roarin' Gulch and descend into the depths of the mine, you'll be taken back to the early 1900s when mining was a way of life.

Best Time to Visit: The World Museum of Mining is open Thursday through Saturday from 10:15 a.m. to 3:00 p.m. The last admission ticket is sold at 2:00 p.m.

Pass/Permit/Fees: General admission to the World Museum of Mining is $9 per person.

Closest City or Town: Butte

Physical Address: 155 Museum Way, Butte, MT 59701

GPS Coordinates: 46.0097° N, 112.5647° W

Did You Know? For $21 per person, you can take the museum's Underground Mine Tour, which will lead you 100 feet into the original shaft of the Orphan Girl Mine.

Amazing Fun Center

The Amazing Fun Center offers the first two-level, human-sized wooden maze in North America. It is located about 7 miles south of Glacier National Park's West Glacier entrance and includes an 18-hole miniature golf course with water features and unique obstacles, a bumper-boat pond, a deluxe go-kart track, and Bankshot Basketball.

The 3D maze is the premier attraction since it's the only one of its kind in the country. Some visitors have taken up to 5 hours to wind their way through the two-level puzzle. This is a fun attraction to visit in groups, especially if you want a variety of activities to choose from.

Best Time to Visit: The Amazing Fun Center is open seasonally through mid-September. Visit between the hours of 9:30 a.m. to 6:00 p.m. from Monday through Thursday and 9:30 a.m. to 7:00 p.m. on Friday and Saturday.

Pass/Permit/Fees: Each activity is priced individually, but a Fun Pass Driver is $25 for visitors ages 13 and up and $22 for visitors ages 6 to 12.

Closest City or Town: Coram

Physical Address: 10265 Highway 2 E, Coram, MT 59912

GPS Coordinates: 48.4252° N, 114.0445° W

Did You Know? The record for completing the two-level maze at the Amazing Fun Center is 21 minutes.

Grant-Kohrs Ranch National Historic Site

This ranch stands as a tribute to the long-gone era of cowboys and cattle herding. One of the last remnants of true American Old West culture, the Grant-Kohrs Ranch used to be the headquarters of a gigantic cattle empire, spanning over 10 million acres. During the 1970s, the National Park Service acquired acreage, rehabilitated parts of the ranch, and added a visitor center and interpretive trails. The site was formally dedicated on July 17, 1977.

This is one of the best places to learn about cattle ranches and their effect on U.S. history. While the industry only lasted about 50 years, it had a huge impact on migrants coming into the area and helped make Montana what it is today.

Best Time to Visit: The best time to visit the Grant-Kohrs Ranch National Historic Site is during the summer.

Pass/Permit/Fees: There is no fee to visit.

Closest City or Town: Deer Lodge

Physical Address: Grant-Kohrs Ranch National Historic Site, 266 Warren Lane, Deer Lodge, MT 59722

GPS Coordinates: 46.4062° N, 112.7367° W

Did You Know? Nearly 100 buildings are preserved from the frontier cattle-ranching era at this location, which is free for visitors to explore.

Big Hole National Battlefield

The Big Hole National Battlefield memorializes and commemorates the battle that took place in 1877 between the Nez Perce and the U.S. Army. After crossing Lolo Pass into Montana, more than 800 Nez Perce and 2,000 horses were traveling through the Bitterroot Valley, believing the military would not engage them despite signs that indicated otherwise. On August 9, the U.S. troops launched a surprise attack on the sleeping Nez Perce. Despite a fierce battle, the Nez Perce eventually fled back to their camp to protect it, realizing that more soldiers were on their way.

Between 60 and 90 Nez Perce men, women, and children died during the battle, along with 31 soldiers and civilian volunteers. The battle represented a turning point in the Flight of 1877, when the Nez Perce were forced to make a 1,170-mile journey over 126 days to their new reservation.

Best Time to Visit: The best time to visit the Big Hole National Battlefield is during the spring, summer, or fall.

Pass/Permit/Fees: There is no fee to visit.

Closest City or Town: Dillon

Physical Address: 16425 Highway 43 West, Wisdom, MT 59761

GPS Coordinates: 45.6455° N, 113.6538° W

Did You Know? The Big Hole National Battlefield includes a visitor center, a film, and a museum to help explain and interpret the events of the battle that was a significant point in Nez Perce history.

Bighorn Canyon Recreation Area

The Bighorn River feeds into this canyon, which contains 55 miles of the 60-mile-wide Bighorn Lake. This recreation area of more than 70,000 acres rests along the border between northern Wyoming and southern Montana. As a result, there are two visitor centers about 3 miles apart. One is in the north near Fort Smith, Montana, and the other is in the south near Lovell, Wyoming.

While the main draw is the world-famous trout fishing, the area also offers the chance to see a variety of wildlife in their natural habitat and walk among them with the camping and hiking opportunities that abound. Boating, kayaking, or canoeing on Bighorn Lake allows you to enjoy awe-inspiring views of the massive canyon walls.

Best Time to Visit: The best time to visit the Bighorn Canyon Recreation Area is during the summer.

Pass/Permit/Fees: As of 2018, a daily pass is no longer needed to enter the location.

Closest City or Town: Fort Smith

Physical Address: Bighorn Canyon National Recreation Area, Fort Smith, MT 59035

GPS Coordinates: 45.3000° N, 107.9768° W

Did You Know? Bighorn Canyon is home to beautiful views, diverse plant and animal life, and Native American historical sites.

Grizzly and Wolf Discovery Center

This wildlife park and educational facility provides visitors with the chance to observe grizzly bears, gray wolves, river otters, and other creatures native to Montana by getting up close and personal with animals that have been rescued or are otherwise unable to survive in the wild. Initially just the Grizzly Discovery Center, this rescue facility opened in 1993 as a way to help visitors better understand grizzlies.

Three years later, the center added ten captive-born wolves and renamed itself the Grizzly and Wolf Discovery Center. In 2019, the Banks of the Yellowstone River Otter Exhibit opened to the public to showcase the connection between Yellowstone's native species across the food chain and natural habitats.

Best Time to Visit: The Grizzly and Wolf Discovery Center is open daily from 9:00 a.m. to 4:00 p.m.

Pass/Permit/Fees: Admission is $15 for adults, $14 for seniors ages 62 and up, and $10 for children ages 5 to 12. Admission is valid for two days.

Closest City or Town: Gardiner

Physical Address: 201 S. Canyon Street, West Yellowstone, MT 59758

GPS Coordinates: 44.6564° N, 111.0986° W

Did You Know? Be sure to visit the *BEARS: Imagination & Reality* museum exhibit that found a permanent home at the center in 2002.

Hebgen Lake

Hebgen Lake is 15 miles long, 4 miles wide, and, surprisingly, only about 70 feet at its deepest. It's a man-made lake retained by an earth-fill dam. The lake and surrounding area offer visitors a variety of activities, including hiking, camping, fishing, and boating.

Two campgrounds are available: Rainbow Point and Cherry Creek. Of the two, Rainbow Point is the larger, offering 20 campsites. Each campsite can fit one full-size camper and one to two accompanying vehicles.

Best Time to Visit: The best time to visit Hebgen Lake is between June and October.

Pass/Permit/Fees: There is no fee to visit.

Closest City or Town: Gardiner

Physical Address: Rainbow Point Campground, Rainbow Point Road, West Yellowstone, MT 59758

GPS Coordinates: 44.8022° N, 111.1811° W

Did You Know? Hebgen Lake is best known for being involved in the large earthquake that created Quake Lake, sealing off the nearby Madison River. The resulting landslide, traveling over 100 mph, caused the waters of Hebgen Lake to be heavily affected.

Quake Lake

Created by an earthquake on August 17, 1959, Quake Lake is only 5 miles long, one-third of a mile wide, and less than 200 feet deep. The most popular activity at the location is fishing from either a boat or the shore. The shoreline is fairly easy to get to; one can access it from Highway 287, and the area has a boat ramp for visitor use.

The Earthquake Lake Visitors Center has a memorial boulder for the 28 people killed by the earthquake, along with a plaque dedicated to them. While there's not a large amount of flora and fauna in the area, fishermen will enjoy a well-stocked lake with a pleasant view.

Best Time to Visit: The best time to visit Quake Lake is during the summer or fall.

Pass/Permit/Fees: There is no fee to visit.

Closest City or Town: Gardiner, Montana

Physical Address:
Earthquake Lake Visitor Center, 317 US-287, Cameron, MT 59720

GPS Coordinates: 44.8317° N, 111.4255° W

Did You Know? The earthquake that created Quake Lake caused a massive landslide involving more than 80 million tons of rock. The landslide stopped the flow of the Madison River in the Madison River Gorge, creating this area.

Yellowstone National Park

Although most of Yellowstone is located in Wyoming, there are areas and trails to explore in the Montana portion of the park too. Known for mountain vistas, forests, and abundant wildlife, the northern edge of Yellowstone in Montana is called the Northern Range.

The Northern Range, the only area of the park that is accessible all year, stretches from Gardiner to Cooke City in Montana. Many drive the 57-mile scenic route between the two cities and stop along the way to explore some of the trails.

Best Time to Visit: The best time to visit Yellowstone National Park is in the summer

Pass/Permit/Fees: Entry fees are $35 per vehicle, $20 per motorcycle, and $20 per individual. Passes are good for 7 days.

Closest City or Town: Gardiner

Physical Address: Gardiner Montana Visitor's Center, 216 Park Street, Gardiner, Montana 59030

GPS Coordinates: 44.4280° N, 110.5885° W

Did You Know? Yellowstone became the first national park on March 1, 1872.

Makoshika State Park

The largest of Montana's state parks, Makoshika covers more than 11,000 acres. It features badland formations and dinosaur fossil remains, and the visitor center at the park entrance has interpretive exhibits. The park is a part of Montana's series of dinosaur-themed museums, state parks, and other attractions called the Montana Dinosaur Trail.

Along with the exhibits, the park offers campgrounds, an archery range, disc golf, an amphitheater, a scenic-drive loop, picnic areas, miles of hiking trails, and incredible scenery.

Best Time to Visit: The best time to visit Makoshika State Park is in the spring, summer, and winter.

Pass/Permit/Fees: Day-use entry fees are $8 per vehicle or $4 for walk-ins. Montana residents who pay the $9 state parks fee with their annual vehicle registration don't have to pay the daily entrance fee.

Closest City or Town: Glendive

Physical Address: Makoshika State Park, 1301 Snyder Street, Glendive, MT 59330

GPS Coordinates: 47.0899° N, 104.7063° W

Did You Know? Over ten different dinosaur species have been discovered in Makoshika State Park, including a complete *Triceratops horridus* skull, the fossil remains of Edmontosaurus and *Tyrannosaurus rex*, and a nearly complete skeleton of the rare Thescelosaur.

Benton Lake National Wildlife Refuge

This wildlife refuge on the western border of the northern Great Plains is fairly small at just 19 square miles, but it's an important wetland habitat for more than 200 bird species and 12 taxonomic orders. More than 6,000 acres of intact northern mixed-grass prairie provide a critical habitat for grassland birds, which are one of the most endangered migratory birds in North America.

These grassland birds include long-billed curlews, burrowing owls, grasshopper sparrows, short-eared owls, chestnut-collared longspurs, Baird's sparrows, sharp-tailed grouses, and others. Visitors may also see mammals such as coyotes, porcupines, American badgers, muskrat, white-tailed deer, pronghorns, and mule deer at various times of the year.

Best Time to Visit: Visit during the spring or fall when the basin is flooded, which attracts many bird species.

Pass/Permit/Fees: There is no fee to visit.

Closest City or Town: Great Falls

Physical Address: Great Falls Visitor Center, 15 Overlook Drive, Great Falls, MT 59405

GPS Coordinates: 47.6871° N, 111.3640° W

Did You Know? Hunting is allowed in the Benton Lake National Wildlife Refuge from September 30 to November 30.

C.M. Russell Museum

With more than 3,000 pieces of Western art in 16 exhibition galleries, you'll need more than just one visit to see everything that the C.M. Russell Museum has to offer. You'll also want to spend some time in the outdoor sculpture garden and immerse yourself in the 1,000 Charles M. Russell art pieces that provide a comprehensive look at Western history.

Plenty of other important artists have works on display that depict the traditions of the North Plains Native Americans, the Montana landscape and wildlife, and "cowboy culture," including Joseph H. Sharp, Winold Reiss, Olaf Wieghorst, and numerous others.

Best Time to Visit: he C.M. Russell Museum is open Wednesday through Monday from May 1 to October 31 and Thursday through Monday from November 1 to April 30. Hours are 10:00 a.m. to 5:00 p.m.

Pass/Permit/Fees: Admission is $14 for adults, $11 for seniors ages 60 and up, and $4 for students over the age of 5. Children ages 5 and under are free.

Closest City or Town: Great Falls

Physical Address: 400 13th Street North, Great Falls, MT 59401

GPS Coordinates: 47.5108° N, 111.2858° W

Did You Know? More than 30,000 people visit the C.M. Russell Museum each year.

Giant Springs State Park

Giant Springs State Park encompasses 14 miles of Missouri River shoreline and provides recreational activities such as fishing, hunting, birdwatching, hiking, biking, photography, boating, and picnicking. The park features one of the largest freshwater springs in the U.S. and the Roe River, which once made *The Guinness Book of World Records* for being the world's shortest river.

Visitors can take a trip through the Giant Springs Fish Hatchery, where they can feed the fish in the show pond, or they can drop a line into the Missouri River or a separate fishing pond. More than 30 miles of paved and dirt trails wander through the park, ranging from easy to difficult. These trails are part of the River's Edge Trail System and connect with 60 miles of trails in the Great Falls region. Four waterfalls are also must-see attractions in the park.

Best Time to Visit: Visit Giant Springs State Park after heavy rain so that the waterfalls are running full.

Pass/Permit/Fees: To enter the park, it is $9 for Montana residents, $8 for nonresident vehicles, and $4 for nonresident walk-ins, bicyclers, or bus passengers.

Closest City or Town: Great Falls

Physical Address: 4803 Giant Springs Road, Great Falls, MT 59405

GPS Coordinates: 47.5347° N, 111.2289° W

Did You Know? The Giant Springs produces more than 156 million gallons of water every day.

Paris Gibson Square Museum of Art

This art museum is housed in the former Great Falls High School, the first high school in the city. The structure was built in 1896, but the high school moved to a new building in 1931. The school then became the Paris Gibson Junior High School until 1975. The Paris Gibson Square Museum of Art moved into the abandoned school in 1977 and focused on showcasing contemporary art by regional artists.

The museum's collection features abstract art, functional art such as jewelry, folk art, and postmodern art. There are two floors of galleries and an outdoor sculpture garden. The museum, like the junior high that preceded it, is named for Paris Gibson, founder of Great Falls, Montana.

Best Time to Visit: The Paris Gibson Square Museum of Art is open Monday, Wednesday, Thursday, and Friday from 10:00 a.m. to 5:00 p.m., Tuesday from 10:00 a.m. to 9:00 p.m., and Saturday from 12:00 p.m. to 5:00 p.m.

Pass/Permit/Fees: There is no fee to visit, but donations are appreciated.

Closest City or Town: Great Falls

Physical Address: 1400 First Avenue North, Great Falls, MT 59401

GPS Coordinates: 47.5069° N, 111.2824°

Did You Know? Just before the museum opened, a planned explosion destroyed the 1913 brick annex for the motion picture *Telefon*.

River's Edge Trail

River's Edge Trail is a paved urban pathway that connects numerous local parks and attractions in Great Falls. It is located on both sides of the Missouri River and provides access to Warden Park, Broadwater Bay, Tourist Park, Riverside Railyard Skate Park, Pacific Steel & Recycling Dog Park, Black Eagle Memorial Island, and several others. It also offers connections to the Lewis & Clark Interpretive Center and the Great Falls Civic Center.

Near the Warden Park gazebo, a telescope gives visitors unparalleled views of Great Falls and the surrounding mountains. Birdwatchers love River's Edge Trail because of the variety of birds that congregate in West Bank Park, particularly around Sacagawea Island.

Best Time to Visit: The River's Edge Trail is available year round but is most comfortable to visit in the warmer weather of spring and summer.

Pass/Permit/Fees: There is no fee to visit.

Closest City or Town: Great Falls

Physical Address: 1700 River Drive North, Great Falls, MT 59403

GPS Coordinates: 47.5193° N, 111.2778° W

Did You Know? The trail is popular for walking, hiking, jogging, skating, cycling, and mountain biking. It offers spectacular views of mountains, prairies, river canyons, waterfalls, reservoirs, and five hydroelectric dams.

The History Museum

The primary purpose of The History Museum in Great Falls is to preserve the culture and history of the north-central Montana Region. It offers a permanent artifact collection and archives and provides educational programming to the community. In addition, the museum acts as a research center for the study of Cascade County history. It has 4,500 square feet of closed stack resources such as photographs, maps, newspapers, blueprints, and yearbooks that the public can access in the Research & Reading Room.

The museum is currently in the process of digitally cataloging its artifacts to allow collections that are not currently on display to be available online. The museum was established in 1976 by the newly formed Cascade County Historical Society, which still operates the museum.

Best Time to Visit: The History Museum is open Tuesday through Friday and every second Saturday of the month from 12:00 p.m. to 5:00 p.m.

Pass/Permit/Fees: There is no fee to visit.

Closest City or Town: Great Falls

Physical Address: 422 2nd Street South, Great Falls, MT 59405

GPS Coordinates: 47.5004° N, 111.3049° W

Did You Know? The History Museum is housed in the former International Harvester building, a 47,625-square-foot structure that was built in 1929.

Blodgett Canyon

Located in Bitterroot National Forest, this scenic canyon was carved out by Ice Age glaciers. It features moraines, steep cliffs, granite mountains, and valleys. The canyon is one of the best big wall-climbing spots in Montana. The South Face of Flathead Buttress is the highest route at about 1,200 feet of sustained vertical.

The Blodgett Canyon Trail is 7 miles out and back. Considered easy, it rewards hikers with a waterfall and spectacular views of the canyon and wilderness. The trail begins at the Canyon Creek trailhead parking lot.

For those who are seeking a backpacking adventure, there is more trail to explore deeper into the canyon too.

Best Time to Visit: The best time to visit Blodgett Canyon is during the summer, fall, and spring.

Pass/Permit/Fees: There is no fee to visit.

Closest City or Town: Hamilton

Physical Address: 1801 N. 1st Street, Hamilton, MT 59840

GPS Coordinates: 46.2738° N, 114.3002° W

Did You Know? The canyon, creek, and mountain in the area are named after Utah immigrants Lyman and Mary Blodgett, who arrived in the area in 1867 in a covered wagon and homesteaded in the Woodside area.

Canyon Ferry Lake

Canyon Ferry Lake has become quite popular over the years because of its location near Helena, Great Falls, and Butte. The reservoir offers many recreational activities, from swimming, boating, and fishing to hunting, camping, and sightseeing. To make it all feasible, boat access has been made available at all campsites, and there are also boat-launch areas near the dam on the north side and Townsend on the south.

In addition to the various activities available, there is a variety of stores and historical buildings for you to explore. Aside from the sapphire mine, you can also learn about Lewis and Clark's passage through the area with Sacagawea.

Best Time to Visit: The best time to visit Canyon Ferry Lake is during the summer or fall.

Pass/Permit/Fees: There is no fee to visit.

Closest City or Town: Helena

Physical Address: Canyon Ferry Reservoir, 7700 Canyon Ferry Road, Helena, MT 59602

GPS Coordinates: 46.4823° N, 111.5446° W

Did You Know? Canyon Ferry Lake is Montana's third-largest body of water. It covers over 35,000 acres and has 76 miles of shore. It was created when Canyon Ferry Dam was built in 1954.

Cathedral of Saint Helena

The first Mass at the Cathedral of Saint Helena was held in 1914 following 5 years of construction on the structure. Bishop John Patrick Carroll was responsible for managing the project. The architect of the cathedral was A.O. Von Herbulis, who was well versed in European cathedrals. He prepared two sketches with proposed styles, one in the Romanesque style and one in the Gothic style.

The Building Committee unanimously selected the Gothic style, and Von Herbulis chose the Votivkirche in Vienna, Austria as the model for the Cathedral of Saint Helena. The cathedral was damaged during the 1935 Helena earthquake and required extensive repairs. It was listed on the National Register of Historic Places in 1980.

Best Time to Visit: Mass services are at 7:00 a.m. from Monday through Friday; 12:00 p.m. on Tuesday and Thursday, 9:00 a.m. on Saturday; and 7:30 a.m., 9:00 a.m., and 11:00 a.m. on Sunday.

Pass/Permit/Fees: There is no fee to visit.

Closest City or Town: Helena

Physical Address: 530 N. Ewing Street, Helena, MT 59601

GPS Coordinates: 46.5909° N, 112.0337° W

Did You Know? The Cathedral of Saint Helena spires are 230 feet tall and adorned with gold-leafed crosses that are each 12 feet in height and 6 feet in length.

ExplorationWorks

ExplorationWorks is an interactive science center that offers entertainment and education for everyone, no matter how old. Exhibits and activities are focused on STEM (science, technology, engineering, and math) principles, which align with educational goals in public schools.

Permanent exhibits include *Waterways to the Future*, which features a water table that depicts Helena's landscape (fire tower, Sleeping Giant Mountain, and Helena Cathedral) and *Little Sky*, a special play area for children under the age of 5 that features Gabriel's Garden Market, the Farm to Fork Barnyard, and the *Montana Outdoors* exhibit. In addition to the permanent exhibits, there is always at least one temporary exhibit that makes each visit unique.

Best Time to Visit: ExplorationWorks is open Tuesday through Sunday from 10:00 a.m. to 5:00 p.m.

Pass/Permit/Fees: General admission is $7.50 for guests ages 2 and up.

Closest City or Town: Helena

Physical Address: 995 Carousel Way, Helena, MT 59601

GPS Coordinates: 46.5985° N, 112.0362° W

Did You Know? Families and schools can rent traveling exhibits from ExplorationWorks, including *Women in Space*, *Shape Your Language*, *Catenary Arch Blocks*, *Simple Machines*, and the *Earthquake Shaker Table*.

Gates of the Mountains Wilderness

A historic site on the Lewis and Clark National Historic Trail, Gates of the Mountains Wilderness is named for the towering limestone walls that the Missouri River carved on one side.

There are 53 miles of well-marked trails, and the most popular trip is Refrigerator Canyon, named for its cool feeling even during the summer. The trail to Refrigerator Canyon is 9 miles and rated moderate. Water is scarce. Motorized and mechanized vehicles, including bicycles, are not allowed in the wilderness, but camping, fishing, and in-season hunting are allowed with the proper permit.

Best Time to Visit: The best time to visit the Gates of the Mountains Wilderness is during the spring, summer, and fall.

Pass/Permit/Fees: No pass, permit, or fee is required except for camping.

Closest City or Town: Helena

Physical Address: 2880 Skyway Drive, Helena, MT 59626

GPS Coordinates: 46.8779° N, 111.9150° W

Did You Know? Lewis and Clark experienced this land by traveling the length of the wilderness via boat on the Missouri River.

Helena National Forest

Named after and headquartered in the capital of Montana, Helena National Forest surrounds the city of Helena and offers nearly 1 million acres of distinctive landscapes. There are 700 miles of hiking trails to explore and over a dozen improved campgrounds throughout the forest, along with a number of trout streams and several lakes.

Crow Creek Falls is often described as the crown jewel of the forest, and the trail is an easy out-and-back hike at 6 miles. The GPS coordinates and directions below will take you to the trailhead.

Best Time to Visit: The best time to visit Helena National Forest is in late spring or summer.

Pass/Permit/Fees: Many recreation sites in the forest require a pass or fee, but there are many free areas too.

Closest City or Town: Helena

Physical Address: 2880 Skyway Drive, Helena, MT 59602

GPS Coordinates: 46.5499° N, 112.2008° W

Did You Know? The Lewis and Clark Expedition of 1804–1806 traveled through many areas of the Helena National Forest, and much of the route looks the same now as it did then.

Holter Museum of Art

Established in 1987 as a space for the local community to experience contemporary art, the Holter Museum of Art has become one of the most celebrated art museums in Montana. There are five exhibition galleries, a collection and research center, and an education center. More than 20 rotating solo and group exhibits are on display every year, making each visit new and exciting. Lectures, receptions, artist residencies, and other opportunities for art education are available each month.

The 17,000-square-foot facility is a significant increase over the initial 10,500 square feet of space that was originally dedicated to showcasing art. This reflects the major growth the museum has experienced during its more than 30 years in existence.

Best Time to Visit: The Holter Museum of Art is open Tuesday through Saturday from 10:00 a.m. to 5:30 p.m. and on Sunday from 12:00 p.m. to 4:00 p.m.

Pass/Permit/Fees: There is no fee to visit.

Closest City or Town: Helena

Physical Address: 12 E. Lawrence Street, Helena, MT 59601

GPS Coordinates: 46.5908° N, 112.0367° W

Did You Know? Since 1987, annual revenues for the Holter Museum of Art have grown from $74,000 to $700,000.

Montana Historical Society

Referred to as the "Guardian of Montana's Memory," the Montana Historical Society was established in 1865 and is one of the oldest organizations of its kind in the Western U.S. In 1969, the society was named the official state archives and repository for the state agency records.

The society's mission is to promote an understanding and appreciation of Montana's past, present, and future cultural heritage. It achieves this mission through its massive collection of art, artifacts, photographs, books, and buildings. Through various educational and public programs, publications, traveling exhibits, and research center, the society brings the state's history alive.

Best Time to Visit: The Montana Historical Society is open Monday through Saturday from 9:00 a.m. to 5:00 p.m.

Pass/Permit/Fees: Admission is $5 for adults and $1 for children. A family can enter for $12 total.

Closest City or Town: Helena

Physical Address: 225 N. Roberts Street, Helena, MT, 59620

GPS Coordinates: 46.5870° N, 112.0163° W

Did You Know? The Moving Images research collection consists of films made by amateur filmmakers, Montana production companies, and Montana state agencies.

Montana State Capitol

In 1889, an election was held to determine where the capital of Montana would be. The cities with the most votes were Helena and Anaconda, but because there was no clear majority, a runoff had to be held. Helena was victorious, and the ground was broken for the new Capitol building in 1895. The capitol's cornerstone was laid on July 4, 1898, but it took until 1901 for the building to be finished.

The massive rotunda is surrounded by four circular paintings surrounding it: a Native American, an explorer and fur trapper, a gold miner, and a cowboy. Other works of art in the building include a semi-elliptical painting, *Driving the Golden Spike*, Charles M. Russell's 1912 painting *Lewis and Clark Meeting the Flathead Indians at Ross' Hole*, and six scenes depicting significant events in early Montana History by Edgar S. Paxson.

Best Time to Visit: The capitol is open for self-guided tours Monday through Friday from 8:00 a.m. to 5:00 p.m.

Pass/Permit/Fees: There is no fee to visit.

Closest City or Town: Helena

Physical Address: 1301 E. 6th Avenue, Helena, MT 59601

GPS Coordinates: 46.5866° N, 112.0186° W

Did You Know? A scavenger hunt for children teaches them about the history of the capitol building. It's led by Lewis and Clark's Newfoundland, Seaman.

Mount Helena City Park

This 620-acre park is home to Mount Helena, which rises 5,468 feet above sea level. Six hiking trails originate in the park and take visitors up and around the mountain. Several of these trails connect to other paths that continue until Helena National Forest. One trail will take you to the Devil's Kitchen cave, and another will take you to the big letter *H* on one side of the mountain.

The easiest trail in the park that will take you to the top of the mountain is the 1906 Trail, which also offers views of Devil's Kitchen and other limestone caves along the way. The longest trail is the Prospector Shafts Trail, which will take you through the southeast quarter of the park and give you views of varied landscapes and abandoned prospector shafts.

Best Time to Visit: The best time to visit Mount Helena City Park is in the summer when the weather is warm.

Pass/Permit/Fees: There is no fee to visit.

Closest City or Town: Helena

Physical Address: Helena Visitor Center, 225 N. Cruse Avenue, Suite A, Helena, MT 59601

GPS Coordinates: 46.5922° N, 112.0589° W

Did You Know? The most challenging trail in Mount Helena City Park is the Powerline Trail.

Original Governor's Mansion

This was once the official residence of the governor of Montana. It was originally built in 1888 by William Chessman and was acquired by the state in 1913. It served as the home for nine Montana governors and their families between 1913 and 1959. The architectural style is Queen Anne, and it was designed by Hodgson, Stem, & Welter of St. Paul, Minnesota.

The 3-story mansion contains 20 rooms and 7 fireplaces. A 2-story brick carriage house is also still standing. Visitors can step back into Montana history by taking a guided tour of the mansion, which has been restored to its original authentic appearance.

Best Time to Visit: Between May 15 and September 15, tours are available Tuesday through Saturday from 12:00 p.m. to 3:00 p.m. Between September 16 and May 14, tours are available on Saturday only between 12:00 p.m. and 3:00 p.m.

Pass/Permit/Fees: Admission is $4 for adults and $1 for children. There is a maximum of $10 in fees per family.

Closest City or Town: Helena

Physical Address: 304 N. Ewing Street, Helena, MT 59601

GPS Coordinates: 46.5883° N, 112.0349° W

Did You Know? The first governor to live in the mansion was Samuel V. Stewart.

Reeder's Alley

Located in historic downtown Helena at the base of Mount Helena, Reeder's Alley was built in the 1870s by Louis Reeder, a Pennsylvania brick and stone mason. The oldest intact remnant of early Helena, the alley provides a glimpse into how the town was settled. It provides insights into the lives of the miners who first came to the area, the Chinese influence on their style, the construction techniques of the 19th century, and the day-to-day activities of the average men and women who traveled to Helena in search of a fortune.

The alley is currently home to several offices and nonprofit organizations, and all buildings in Reeder's Alley are listed on the National Register of Historic Places. Reeder's Alley was donated to the Montana Heritage Commission in 2000 to ensure it is properly preserved.

Best Time to Visit: The best time to visit Reeder's Alley is during the day so that the architectural details can be adequately appreciated.

Pass/Permit/Fees: There is no fee to visit.

Closest City or Town: Helena

Physical Address: 101 Reeder's Alley, Helena, MT 59601

GPS Coordinates: 46.5858° N, 112.0434° W

Did You Know? Reeder's Alley was originally named Cutler Street in Last Chance Gulch when it was established after the discovery of gold in 1864.

Spring Meadow Lake State Park

This day-use state park is a popular getaway for swimming, fishing, birdwatching, and sunbathing. You're sure to glimpse rabbits and turtles in the park, among many other animals. Anglers enjoy Spring Meadow Lake for its abundance of bass, sunfish, and trout, and the ADA-accessible fishing dock added in 2011 just makes it even easier for fishermen to participate in their favorite pastime.

In the winter, the lake freezes over and becomes a wonderful place for ice skating and ice fishing. While no dogs are allowed at the park in the summer, they are welcome between October 16 and April 14 when fewer people are visiting the area.

Best Time to Visit: The best time to visit Spring Meadow Lake State Park is in the summer for swimming, fishing, birdwatching, and sunbathing or in the winter for ice skating and ice fishing.

Pass/Permit/Fees: There is no fee to visit.

Closest City or Town: Helena

Physical Address: 2715 Country Club Drive, Helena, MT 59601

GPS Coordinates: 46.6123° N, 112.0753° W

Did You Know? Spring Meadow Lake is a man-made lake fed by a natural spring with clean, cool water. Until the 1980s, the area was an active gravel pit.

Tizer Botanic Gardens & Arboretum

The Tizer Botanic Gardens & Arboretum offers 6 acres of spectacular gardens that can be accessed by various trails that total approximately half a mile. The gorgeous gardens include a rose garden, vegetable garden, herb garden, children's garden, shade garden, gazebo garden, secret garden, butterfly and hummingbird garden, meditation garden, and more.

A wildflower walk that blooms during the spring and summer gives visitors a glimpse of some of Montana's most incredible wildflowers, such as buttercups, sugar bowls, and crocus. An observation deck along the walk allows visitors to sit quietly while they enjoy the breathtaking view.

Best Time to Visit: The Tizer Botanic Gardens & Arboretum is open daily from 10:00 a.m. to 6:00 p.m.

Pass/Permit/Fees: Admission is $9 for adults and $7 for children ages 5 to 12, and free for children under the age of 5.

Closest City or Town: Jefferson City

Physical Address: 38 Tizer Lake Road, Jefferson City, MT 59638

GPS Coordinates: 46.3731° N, 112.0231° W

Did You Know? The Tizer Botanic Gardens & Arboretum opened in 1997 as the vision of Richard Krott and Belva Lotzer. Last year, more than 15,000 guests visited the gardens.

Artemis Acres Paint Horse Ranch

The full Montana experience can be had at the Artemis Acres Guest Ranch, a Western lodging facility in the foothills of the Salish Mountain Range in Kalispell. The 80-acre property and adjacent leased land provide miles of trails for hiking and horseback riding. Traditional Western meals are served for breakfast and dinner, including savory meats and plenty of fresh fruits and vegetables.

The ranch is just 30 miles from Glacier National Park and 8 miles from Flathead Lake, so it's the perfect location for exploring some of the best recreational areas Montana has to offer. You can also relax at the ranch or take a hike into the surrounding forests. The guided horseback rides take you through miles of timberland and mountain forests.

Best Time to Visit: Visit during the summer when the horseback trails are clear.

Pass/Permit/Fees: The cost depends on the dates and length of your stay. Check the website for pricing details.

Closest City or Town: Kalispell

Physical Address: 610 Patrick Creek Road, Kalispell, MT 59901

GPS Coordinates: 48.1142° N, 114.3302° W

Did You Know? The Artemis Acres Paint Horse Ranch is owned by Cecil and Isabel Noble, who have a combined 46 years of backcountry horseback riding and guiding.

Flathead Lake

With over 185 miles of shoreline and 200 square miles of water, Flathead Lake is the largest natural freshwater lake west of the Mississippi in the lower 48 states. The lake is perfect for a myriad of recreational activities, including swimming, fishing, kayaking, boating, and other watersports. Thirteen public access sites maintained by the Montana Fish Wildlife and Parks have full amenities.

Various trails can be explored near the lake, including the Flathead Lake Interpretive Trail, which takes hikers a short, steep distance of 0.4 miles down to the eastern shore of the lake and back in a loop.

Best Time to Visit: The best time to visit Flathead Lake is during the summer.

Pass/Permit/Fees: A tribal recreation permit is required.

Closest City or Town: Kalispell

Physical Address: Flathead Lake State Park, 28031 Big Arm State Park Road, Big Arm, MT 59910

GPS Coordinates: 47.9056° N, 114.1156° W

Did You Know? Folklore talks of a large eel-shaped creature being spotted in the lake, and residents have nicknamed it "Flessie," inspired by the Loch Ness's "Nessie."

Hockaday Museum of Art

Originally named the Hockaday Center for the Arts and designed as a community art center when it opened in 1969, the Hockaday Museum of Art was renamed in 1998 to reflect its primary purpose as a collecting museum. The permanent collection at the museum includes art with a focus on Montana and Glacier National Park. Some artists whose works are included in the collection are Ace Powell, Doug Winton, Rebecca Tobey, and Hugh Hockaday.

The museum is housed in the Carnegie Library Building, a 125-year-old structure that has been extensively renovated to be ADA compliant and create an upscale museum environment. However, the building's historic beauty remains intact.

Best Time to Visit: The Hockaday Museum of Art is open Tuesday from 11:00 a.m. to 5:00 p.m. and Wednesday through Saturday from 11:00 a.m. to 4:00 p.m.

Pass/Permit/Fees: Admission is $5 for adults $4 for seniors over the age of 60, and $2 for college students. Children are free.

Closest City or Town: Kalispell

Physical Address: 302 2nd Avenue East, Kalispell, MT 59901

GPS Coordinates: 48.1969° N, 114.3102° W

Did You Know? The Hockaday Museum of Art is named for Hugh Hockaday, an original founding member of the Flathead Valley Art Association.

Swan Lake

While Swan Lake isn't very large compared to many of Montana's other lakes, it's as worth visiting as any other. This 8-mile-long lake is only about a mile wide, but it's become a popular fishing and resort area.

In addition, the U.S. Forest Service day-use area offers a variety of amenities, including public toilets, an eating area with picnic tables, and even a small beach, complete with boat dock. Great for a family day trip or even a weekend of camping, there's something for all to enjoy at Swan Lake.

Best Time to Visit: The best time to visit Swan Lake is during the summer or fall.

Pass/Permit/Fees: There is no fee to visit.

Closest City or Town: Kalispell

Physical Address: Swan Lake Campground, Swan Lake, MT 59911

GPS Coordinates: 47.9291° N, 113.8448° W

Did You Know? You can see the peaks of the Swan Mountain Range from the lake. The lake may have been named for the range; for Emmett Swan, an early resident of the area; or for the trumpeter swans that used to populate the lake.

Wild Horse Island State Park

This is the largest island in Flathead Lake, Montana's largest freshwater lake. Its scenic shoreline is popular with hikers, boaters, swimmers, and sailboat enthusiasts. Access is only by boat and for day-use only.

A recommended public access point is at Skeeko Bay on the north side of the island, where there are places to dock your boat and access the trails. In addition to a few wild horses, the park is home to a variety of wildlife, including bighorn sheep, mule deer, songbirds, waterfowl, bald eagles, and falcons.

Best Time to Visit: The best time to visit Wild Horse Island State Park is in the summer.

Pass/Permit/Fees: The day-use entry fee is $8 for vehicles and $4 for walk-ins. Montana residents who pay the $9 state park fee with their vehicle registration don't have to pay daily entrance fees.

Closest City or Town: Kalispell

Physical Address: 490 North Meridian Road, Kalispell, MT 59901

GPS Coordinates: 47.8461° N, 114.2179° W

Did You Know? Wild Horse Island has been a landmark since the Salish-Kootenai Indians were reported to have used it to pasture horses to keep them from being stolen by other tribes.

American Prairie Reserve

Located in central Montana, the American Prairie Reserve spans the Great Plains of Montana north and south of the Missouri River. The region is one of the most remote areas of the lower 48 states.

Most of the visitor facilities are located on the PN, Mars Vista, and Sun Prairie property areas of the reserve, which include campgrounds and a hut system. The Mars Vista is accessible in all kinds of weather with all vehicle types, while other properties require higher-profile, 4WD vehicles. The recently opened National Discovery Center in Lewistown is within a short drive of the prairie. It will eventually host local, regional, and national activities as well as programs geared toward preservation of the prairie.

Best Time to Visit: The best time to visit the American Prairie Reserve is during spring, summer, and fall.

Pass/Permit/Fees: There is no fee to visit.

Closest City or Town: Lewiston

Physical Address: Lewistown Visitor Center, 408 E. Main Street, Lewistown, MT 59457

GPS Coordinates: 47.7448° N, 107.7758° W

Did You Know? The American Prairie Reserve continues to acquire land and grow. When complete, APR will span more than 3 million acres.

Crystal Cascades

Crystal Cascades trail lies below Crystal Lake in the Snowy Mountains, running alongside Rock Creek for most of the trail. It's a 7-mile out-and-back trail, with approximately 1,000 feet in elevation gain from the trailhead to the cascades themselves. Overall, the trail is moderately difficult, as there are many stream crossings.

These areas are where you should be the most cautious because they often require the hiker to move across slick surfaces. Terrain can vary widely. Wet logs and rocks are common, and there are steep sections. The trail runs through dense forest with fairly heavy undergrowth and is almost entirely shaded, so it's a great hike on a hot day, but a jacket is recommended on cooler days.

Best Time to Visit: If snow is not preferred, then either July or August are ideal months to visit the trail.

Pass/Permit/Fees: It costs $10 a night to camp, but day entry is free.

Closest City or Town: Lewistown

Physical Address: Crystal Falls Trailhead, Crystal Lake Road, Moore, MT 59464

GPS Coordinates: 46.7950° N, 109.4818° W

Did You Know? Crystal Cascades Trail is home to a 100-foot-high waterfall.

Kootenai Falls

Kootenai Falls and the surrounding area offer a breathtaking view as the Kootenai River loses about 300 feet in elevation down the river. Located inside Kootenai National Forest, the Kootenai is the largest undammed waterfall in Montana and also one of the largest by flow rate in the country.

The main waterfall, which is 30 feet high, can be viewed from a swinging bridge that crosses the river. Kootenai Falls is considered sacred to the Kootenai tribe, and the area features a river, the falls, and rock cliffs. Hunting, fishing, swimming, and wildlife viewing are popular activities in the area

Best Time to Visit: The best time to visit Kootenai Falls is between June and September.

Pass/Permit/Fees: There is no fee to visit.

Closest City or Town: Libby

Physical Address: Kootenai National Forest, 31374 US Highway 2, Libby, MT 59923-3022

GPS Coordinates: 48.4537° N, 115.7691° W

Did You Know? Kootenai Falls has been featured in two movies: *River Wild* from 1994 and *The Revenant* from 2015.

Paradise Valley

One of the most scenic valleys in Montana, this river valley links Livingston to Gardiner. Nestled between two mountain ranges, it offers various places to visit and enjoy the wilderness and scenery.

Pine Creek Trail, which hikes to Pine Creek Falls, is 2.5 miles out and back to the falls. The trail continues for another 4 miles and gains elevation on its way to an alpine lake. There is also the 62-mile Paradise Scenic Loop Drive with several stops for more adventure. One notable stop along the loop is The Gallatin Forest Interpretive Trail in the Tom Miner Basin, which is 8 miles long and rated moderate.

Best Time to Visit: The best time to visit Paradise Valley is during the spring, summer, or fall.

Pass/Permit/Fees: There is no fee to visit.

Closest City or Town: Livingston

Physical Address: Pine Creek Campground, 266 Luccock Park Road, Livingston, MT 59047

GPS Coordinates: 45.4986° N, 110.5189° W

Did You Know? Paradise Valley is also known for world-class fly fishing in the Yellowstone River and creeks throughout the area.

Lolo Trail

Lolo Trail is a Historic National Trail that brought many travelers over the Bitterroot Mountains, including the Lewis and Clark Expedition. It is a network of trails rather than a single path, offering a multi-day adventure.

On the border of Montana and Idaho, Lolo Pass is the highest point of the historic trail and a great place for a scenic drive. Howard Creek has a 0.4-mile loop that includes part of the original trail, and there is a longer section of the trail to hike at Lee Creek Campground.

Best Time to Visit: The best time to visit the Lolo Trail is between July and September.

Pass/Permit/Fees: No fee is required.

Closest City or Town: Lola

Physical Address: Lolo Pass Visitor Center, 44000 US-12, Lolo, MT 59847

GPS Coordinates: 46.6352° N, 114.5798° W

Did You Know? The Lolo Trail was the northern route across the rugged Bitterroot Mountains used by Native Americans for centuries before Lewis and Clark. The Nez Perce used it while traveling east to the Great Plains and buffalo, and the Salish used it to reach the Lochsa River, where they fished for salmon.

Bob Marshall Wilderness

A small part of a much larger wilderness complex, the Bob Marshall Wilderness is a sight to behold. Saved by its namesake, the forester Bob Marshall, this is a nearly untouched region that was set aside to be protected back in 1941, along with other areas saved by Marshall.

Because of his efforts, this is one of the best-preserved mountainous regions in the world, offering beautiful, natural views of gently sloping alpine meadows, rugged ridge tops, open grass parks, and thickly forested river bottoms. Visit with the family any time during the summer and you'll have more options than needed for a fun family outing.

Best Time to Visit: The best time to visit the Bob Marshall Wilderness is during the summer.

Pass/Permit/Fees: There is no fee to visit.

Closest City or Town: Missoula

Physical Address: Flathead National Forest, 650 Wolf Pack Way, Kalispell, MT 59901

GPS Coordinates: 46.9311° N, 112.9745° W

Did You Know? This is one of the last safe areas for grizzly bears and other animals such as the gray wolves.

Caras Park

Caras Park is situated along the Clark Fork River in downtown Missoula. Along with the Caras Park Pavilion, this location is a spectacular venue for public and private events. More than 1,000 events have been hosted at the park over its 12-year existence, including Out to Lunch, the Missoula Marathon Expo, Downtown ToNight, the International Wildlife Film Festival's WildFest, Celtic Fest, Parks & Recreation's Kid Fest, First Night Missoula, Garden City BrewFest, and GermanFest, among others.

Caras Park is also home to an old-fashioned carousel that features handcrafted horses, all of which have fun names like Columbia Belle, Moonlight, Montana Appaloosa, Midnight Rose, Sweet Sue, and more. There's even a dragon ring machine that drops rings for riders to grab. Anyone who grabs a brass ring gets a free carousel ride.

Best Time to Visit: The best time to visit Caras Park is during an event, most of which occur in the summer. Check the website for dates and times.

Pass/Permit/Fees: There is no fee to visit, but there may be a fee to attend a specific event.

Closest City or Town: Missoula

Physical Address: 123 Carousel Drive, Missoula, MT 59802

GPS Coordinates: 46.8694° N, 113.9972° W

Did You Know? Nearly 1 million people have visited Caras Park throughout its dozen years of operation.

Clark Fork Riverfront Trail

The Clark Fork Riverfront Trail connects city parks, neighborhoods, open spaces, businesses, and the University of Montana in Missoula. The trail is designed for walking, bicycling, and horseback riding (although not in every area). It extends from west of downtown Missoula to Hellgate Canyon, which is east of the city.

Three street bridges cross the Clark Fork of the Columbia River: one on Orange Street, one on Higgins Avenue, and one on Madison Street. A footbridge just off Van Buren Street allows for easy access to the University of Montana Campus. A second footbridge is located off California Street. The Clark Fork Riverfront Trail also connects with various other trails that lead to recreational areas including the Patee Canyon Recreation Area and the Rattlesnake National Recreation Area and Wilderness.

Best Time to Visit: The trail can be used daily from sunrise to sunset.

Pass/Permit/Fees: There is no fee to visit.

Closest City or Town: Missoula

Physical Address: Missoula Walk-In Visitor Center, 101 E. Main Street, Missoula, MT 59802

GPS Coordinates: 48.1854° N, 116.2692° W

Did You Know? More than 40 trails are part of the Clark Fork Riverfront Trail system.

Lolo National Forest

There are more than 2 million acres in Lolo National Forest, many of which are used for recreational activities such as camping, hiking, cross-country skiing, four wheeling, horseback riding, biking, birdwatching, kayaking, snowmobiling, and more. Located in western Montana and bordering Idaho, the forest encompasses four wilderness areas: the Welcome Creek, Rattlesnake, Scapegoat, and Selway-Bitterroot wildernesses.

The forest has formally existed since 1906, but four separate forests existed well before that year and were combined into the single Lolo National Forest for administrative reasons. There are at least 12 campgrounds within the forest and more than 700 miles of hiking trails, along with 100 named lakes and 5 rivers.

Best Time to Visit: Visit any time of year.

Pass/Permit/Fees: There is a fee of $5 per day to visit the forest, or a season pass can be purchased for $35.

Closest City or Town: Missoula

Physical Address: 25 Fort Missoula Road, Missoula, MT 59804

GPS Coordinates: 47.58986 N, 115.57780 W

Did You Know? The Lolo National Forest has the largest western red cedar trees in the state at more than 8 feet in diameter and 200 feet in height.

Mission Valley-Mission Mountain Wilderness

The Mission Mountain Wilderness is a fairly large area made up of almost 74,000 acres of well-preserved natural beauty for visitors to explore at their leisure. A few mountains rise to elevations as high as 9,000 feet, with McDonald Peak reaching 9,820 feet.

In addition to signs of both black bears and grizzly bears, you can see all kinds of wildlife in the Mission Mountain Wilderness area, including mountain goats, elk, deer, various predators, and a variety of bird species.

Best Time to Visit: The best time to visit Mission Valley is before July or after October.

Pass/Permit/Fees: Call the Flathead National Forest for permit information.

Closest City or Town: Missoula

Physical Address: Flathead National Forest, 650 Wolfpack Way, Kalispell, MT 59901

GPS Coordinates: 47.2234° N, 113.5553° W

Did You Know? The Mission Mountain Wilderness is in the Rocky Mountains. A section is closed to most visitors for part of the year because grizzlies tend to gather in the snow fields to feast on a variety of bugs, namely cutworm moths and ladybugs.

Missoula Art Museum

The Missoula Art Museum has roots in the 1972 Festival of the Arts, which was attended by more than 10,000 people, illustrating the need for an art museum in the city. The Missoula Museum of the Arts opened in 1975.

Housed in the former home of the Missoula Free Public Library, which was built in 1903, the museum completed a complete renovation of the building between 2005 and 2006. It fused the century-old Carnegie Library with a contemporary wing that is the perfect space for exhibiting, celebrating, and preserving the museum's contemporary art collection. When the newly renovated museum reopened, it was under the new Missoula Art Museum name. In 2017, the museum expanded once again with the addition of Art Park, its outdoor sculpture park that features seasonally appropriate large-scale sculptures.

Best Time to Visit: The Missoula Art Museum is open Tuesday through Saturday from 10:00 a.m. to 5:00 p.m.

Pass/Permit/Fees: There is no fee to visit.

Closest City or Town: Missoula

Physical Address: 335 N. Pattee Street, Missoula, MT 59802

GPS Coordinates: 46.8731° N, 113.9924° W

Did You Know? The first exhibition shown at the Missoula Art Museum was *Native Funk and Flash,* which reflected the avant-garde trend of the 1970s.

Missoula Downtown and Hip Strip

If you're looking for a unique shopping area to find uncommon gifts for those hard-to-shop-for friends and loved ones, you're sure to enjoy the Hip Strip in Downtown Missoula. All shops are 100 percent locally owned and operated, so there won't be any chain stores here. You'll discover clothing, books, music, art, and even surfboards in this collection of boutique shops and stores.

Nestled among these eclectic establishments are local restaurants, bakeries, ice cream shops, coffee shops, and even a brewery, so if you need a break from shopping, stop in and grab a meal or treat. Some of the most popular shops along the Hip Strip are Ear Candy Music, Bathing Beauties Beads, Meadowsweet Herbs, Shakespeare & Co., Strongwater MTN Surf Co., and The Art Hang Up.

Best Time to Visit: The best time to visit the Hip Strip is during the summer when most stores have expanded operating hours.

Pass/Permit/Fees: There is no fee to visit, but be sure to bring money for when you find those perfect gifts.

Closest City or Town: Missoula

Physical Address: Intersection of Brooks Street and Higgins Avenue, Missoula, MT 59801

GPS Coordinates: 46.8637° N, 113.9973° W

Did You Know? The Hip Strip is also home to a teen-friendly dance venue called the Legacy Lounge, which offers live music, DJs, and dancing but no alcohol.

Mount Sentinel

Mount Sentinel, originally named Mount Woody, is a relatively small mountain located east of the University of Montana in Missoula. The most prominent feature of Mount Sentinel is a white concrete letter *M* located 620 feet up the side of the mountain.

The University of Montana has owned about 40 acres of land on Mount Sentinel since 1902 when the Northern Pacific Railroad Company donated it to the school. The City of Missoula also owns approximately 475 acres on the face of the mountain. The first *M* on the side of the mountain was built in 1909 out of whitewashed rocks, and the freshman class re-created it out of wood in 1912. The concrete structure was installed in 1968 because it became too difficult to maintain the rock *M*.

Best Time to Visit: The best time to visit Mount Sentinel is during homecoming weekend when UM students make the annual trek up the mountain to "light the *M*."

Pass/Permit/Fees: There is no fee to visit.

Closest City or Town: Missoula

Physical Address: 1111–1201 Campus Drive, Missoula, MT 59812

GPS Coordinates: 46.8552° N, 113.9643° W

Did You Know? When the University of Montana was gifted 40 acres of land at the base and slope of Mount Sentinel, it became the only university in the U.S. to own a mountain.

National Bison Range

This wildlife refuge and nature reserve, located on the Flathead Indian Reservation, is devoted to the conservation of American bison. The range has large hills and small mountains and is home to 350–500 bison in addition to many other mammal species such as mule deer, elk, bighorn sheep, and pronghorn.

Most of the refuge can be explored via Red Sleep Drive, a 19-mile scenic drive, but there are four trails available: Nature Trail (1 mile), Grassland Trail (0.25 miles), Bitterroot Trail (0.5 miles), and High Point Trail (1 mile). These are all easy trails. Fishing is allowed in designated areas with a license.

Best Time to Visit: The best time to visit is from June to September when the weather is warmer.

Pass/Permit/Fees: There is a $10 day-use fee per car, but you can also purchase an annual pass for $20.

Closest City or Town: Missoula

Physical Address: 58355 Bison Range Road, Charlo, MT 59824

GPS Coordinates: 47.3707° N, 114.2570° W

Did You Know? The National Bison Range was originally established in 1908 on land taken without the consent of the Flathead tribe. The bison herd is descended from a free-ranging herd started by tribal members in the 1800s. The land was restored in 2020 to federal trust ownership for the

Confederated Salish and Kootenai tribes, who now operate as stewards of the range's land, buffalo, and other wildlife.

Rattlesnake National Recreation Area

Located in the Rattlesnake Mountains, this national recreation area is a popular destination in the Missoula Valley. It is known for its forested ridges, cliff-banded slopes, and scenic lakes. The peak elevation in the area is 8,620 feet at the top of McLeod Peak. Favorite activities in the recreation area include mountain biking, hiking, fishing, horseback riding, camping, hunting, cross-country skiing, and snowshoeing.

The Route of the Hiawatha is an educational and historic bike route that passes through the recreation area and into Idaho. Expect to see bighorn sheep, deer, and owls in the park, along with many bird species.

Best Time to Visit: The best time to visit Rattlesnake National Recreation Area depends on the activity you're participating in. Biking, hiking, fishing, and camping are great in the spring and summer, while cross-country skiing and snowshoeing are only available in the winter.

Pass/Permit/Fees: There is no fee to visit.

Closest City or Town: Missoula

Physical Address: 24 Fort Missoula Road, Missoula, MT 59804

GPS Coordinates: 46.9670° N, 113.8717° W

Did You Know? More than 30 mountain lakes in Rattlesnake National Recreation Area have been created from melting glaciers.

Rocky Mountain Elk Foundation Visitor Center

With more than 231,000 members, the Rocky Mountain Elk Foundation is one of the largest conservation and hunting heritage organizations in the U.S. More than 13,000 projects have protected or enhanced over 8.2 million acres of wildlife habitat. The 12,000 volunteers in 500 chapters have also worked to improve public access to at least 1.3 million acres, most of which were previously off limits to the public.

The foundation continues to be a vocal advocate for elk, elk habitat, hunters, public access, wildlife management, and conservation programs all over the country.

Best Time to Visit: The Rocky Mountain Elk Foundation Visitor Center is open Monday through Friday from 8:00 a.m. to 5:00 p.m. and Saturday and Sunday from 9:00 a.m. to 5:00 p.m.

Pass/Permit/Fees: There is no fee to visit.

Closest City or Town: Missoula

Physical Address: 5705 Grant Creek Road, Missoula, MT 59808

GPS Coordinates: 46.9194° N, 114.0327° W

Did You Know? Four elk hunters from northwest Montana established the Rocky Mountain Elk Foundation in 1984 when they realized there were no organizations dedicated to protecting the future of elk.

St. Francis Xavier Church

It's the tallest church in Missoula, so you won't be able to miss historic St. Francis Xavier Church, with its century-old paintings and Romanesque Revival architecture. The church was constructed in 1892 following the vision of Father Diomedi, SJ, who realized the area needed a bigger church than the chapel that was then serving Missoula.

The new church was designed to hold 600 worshippers on the main floor and 150 more in the choir loft. The paintings were done by a kitchen helper named Joseph Carignano, who created them in his spare time. In addition to Carignano's gorgeous paintings, the church also features stained-glass windows; a 2,270-pound bell; and a pipe organ.

Best Time to Visit: The best time to visit St. Francis Xavier Church is during Mass, which is held Monday through Friday at 8:00 a.m.; Saturday at 5:00 p.m.; and Sunday at 8:00 a.m., 10:00 a.m., and 6:00 p.m.

Pass/Permit/Fees: There is no fee to visit.

Closest City or Town: Missoula

Physical Address: 420 W. Pine Street, Missoula, MT 59802

GPS Coordinates: 46.8754° N, 113.9981° W

Did You Know? Joseph Carignano, who painted the interior of St. Francis Xavier Church, also painted the frescoes at St. Ignatius Mission.

The Historical Museum at Fort Missoula

Located on 32 acres, the Historical Museum at Fort Missoula gives visitors a glimpse into the fascinating history of western Montana. The scope of the museum ranges from the establishment of the fort in 1877 during the Indian Wars to the All-African American 25th Infantry Bicycle Corps in the late 1800s to the World War II internment camp that was the forced home of more than 2,200 Italian and Japanese nationals.

There are more than 20 historical structures on the grounds, and the museum features rotating exhibits about historical subjects that are engaging for visitors of all ages. In addition, the museum hosts various educational events throughout the year.

Best Time to Visit: The museum is open Tuesday through Sunday from 12:00 p.m. to 5:00 p.m. from Labor Day to Memorial Day. For the rest of the year, it's open Monday through Saturday from 10:00 a.m. to 5:00 p.m. and on Sunday from 12:00 p.m. to 5:00 p.m.

Pass/Permit/Fees: Admission is $4 for adults, $3 for seniors, and $2 for students. There is a maximum fee of $10 per family.

Closest City or Town: Missoula

Physical Address: 3400 Captain Rawn Way, Missoula, MT 59804

GPS Coordinates: 46.84439 N, 114.06289 W

Did You Know? Of the many WWII incarceration sites in the U.S., Fort Missoula has the most intact one remaining.

The Historic Wilma Theatre

Locally known as "the Wilma," the Historic Wilma Theatre was built in 1921 as a tribute to Edna Wilma, a light opera artist who was married to William "Billy" Simons, the principal builder. The Wilma is housed in an 8-story building that was the first steel-framed high-rise structure in Missoula. The theater's 1,400-seat hall joins three banquet rooms, a lounge, apartments, offices, and a restaurant that are also located in this historic building.

The Wilma offers a wide range of entertainment, including independent movies, stand-up comedy shows, spoken-word events, live and local music shows, plays, and more. The theater is considered Missoula's entertainment hub and hosts two world-famous film festivals each year.

Best Time to Visit: The best time to visit the Historic Wilma Theatre is when a show is playing that you want to see. Check the website for show dates and times.

Pass/Permit/Fees: The cost to visit depends on show and seat selection.

Closest City or Town: Missoula

Physical Address: 131 Higgins Avenue, Missoula, MT 59802

GPS Coordinates: 46.8702° N, 113.9961° W

Did You Know? While home to vaudeville shows when it first opened, the Wilma served mostly as a movie house until the 1980s when live entertainment made it on stage.

Pryor Mountains

This mountain range is located in Carbon and Big Horn counties in Montana and on the Crow Indian Reservation and the Chief Plenty Coups State Park. The Pryor Mountains span 145,000 square miles and pass into parts of Wyoming. Limestone caves that were carved by groundwater dot the landscape throughout the area. The best-known caves are the Mystery Cave and the Big Ice Cave. Others include False Cougar Cave, which Native Americans used for various purposes, Little Ice Cave, Shield Trap Cave, and Bell Trap Cave.

Other features include Froggs Fault (a giant fissure in the surface) and Buffalo Jump near Dry Head Lookout, a small indention in the cliff face that's surrounded by a fence of rock.

Best Time to Visit: The best time to visit the Pryor Mountains is in the summer when the weather is better.

Pass/Permit/Fees: There is no fee to visit.

Closest City or Town: Pryor

Physical Address: Chief Plenty Coups State Park, 1 Pryor Road, Pryor, MT 59066

GPS Coordinates: 45.1708° N, 108.3361° W

Did You Know? The Pryor Mountains are named for Sergeant Nathaniel Hale Pryor, who was a member of the Lewis and Clark Expedition.

Beartooth Highway

One of the most scenic drives in the U.S., Beartooth Highway is an All-American Road located on a section of U.S. Route 212. This National Scenic Byway is a 68-mile corridor that begins and ends in Montana, ranging from the entrance to Yellowstone National Park near Cooke City to Red Lodge. A large portion extends into Wyoming.

Beartooth Highway travels through the Custer, Shoshone, and Gallatin national forests, reaching elevations of over 10,000 feet. There are multiple places to stop and hike, camp, fish, and admire the scenery. Top of the World Store sits at about 9,400 feet in elevation along Beartooth Highway and Resort. It offers supplies, souvenirs, beverages, and gas.

Best Time to Visit: Beartooth Highway is open briefly in the spring and summer depending on weather conditions.

Pass/Permit/Fees: There is no fee to visit.

Closest City or Town: Red Lodge

Physical Address: Red Lodge Visitor's Center, 701 North Broadway, Red Lodge, Montana 59068

GPS Coordinates: 44.9392° N, 109.6136° W

Did You Know? Although it's short compared to other scenic drives in the U.S., Beartooth Highway winds its way through 20 peaks and past glaciers, mountain lakes, and three national forests.

Granite Peak

At 12,807 feet above sea level, Granite Peak is the highest natural point in the state of Montana. This summit is considered to be one of the most difficult of the 50-state high points. It's at least a 2-day climb, with an overnight stay on the scary-sounding Froze-to-Death Plateau.

The main trail to the summit is strenuous at 10–12 miles one way with sections of exposed class 3 and 4 rock climbing. A rope, harness, slings, and a rappel device are recommended for those not comfortable with extreme exposure. The standard route to take is South Face via East Ridge on the West Rosebud/Mystic Lake Trail, but there are multiple ways to approach the summit.

Best Time to Visit: The best time to visit Granite Peak Trail is between April and September.

Pass/Permit/Fees: There is no fee to visit.

Closest City or Town: Red Lodge

Physical Address: Mystic Lake Trailhead, W. Rosebud Lake Road, Fishtail, MT 59028

GPS Coordinates: 45.2457° N, 109.7297° W

Did You Know? In recent years, the Southwest Couloir Route has gained popularity because it is a nontechnical option.

Grinnell Glacier

Grinnell Glacier trail is a fairly long but popular out-and-back trail, featuring a lake with a pair of shuttle boats that you may take (for a fee) to shorten the route by about 3.5 miles. Many people choose this, but it is not necessary because the entire trail is well maintained.

The option that uses the shuttles will first take you from Many Glacier Hotel across Swiftcurrent Lake. The next boat will ferry you across Lake Josephine, where you may continue the hike.

Best Time to Visit: The best time to visit Grinnell Glacier is between August and October.

Pass/Permit/Fees: The summer rate is $35 per vehicle, and the winter rate is $25 per vehicle.

Closest City or Town: Siyeh Bend

Physical Address: Glacier National Park, 64 Grinnell Drive, West Glacier, MT 59936

GPS Coordinates: 48.7513° N, 113.7278° W

Did You Know? The glacier was named after George Bird Grinnell, an early American conservationist and explorer who strongly advocated for the creation of Glacier National Park.

First Peoples Buffalo Jump State Park

The First Peoples Buffalo Jump State Park is a National Historic Landmark and archaeological site. It's also the location of the largest bison cliff jump in North America.

The bison jump is a mile-long sandstone cliff that was used by Native Americans for at least 1,000 years before Lewis and Clark began exploring the area. Visitors can see drive lines on top of the cliff and up to 18 feet of packed buffalo remains below. The education center offers buffalo culture exhibits, a gallery, a storytelling circle, and a bookstore.

Best Time to Visit: The park is open daily from 8:00 a.m. to 6:00 p.m. in the summer. In the winter, it's open Wednesday through Saturday from 10:00 a.m. to 4:00 p.m. and Sunday from 12:00 p.m. to 4:00 p.m.

Pass/Permit/Fees: The day-use entry fee is $8 for vehicles and $4 for walk-ins. Montana residents who pay the $9 state park fee with their vehicle registration don't have to pay daily entrance fees.

Closest City or Town: Ulm

Physical Address: 342 Ulm-Vaughn Road, Ulm, MT 59485

GPS Coordinates: 47.4802° N, 111.5247° W

Did You Know? The buffalo jump at this state park was used by horseless Native Americans to drive bison over a cliff. Once the bison jumped over the cliff, they would be killed for their meat, bones, and hides.

Avalanche Lake

The hike to Avalanche Lake is one of the most popular hikes in Glacier National Park because of the stunning views throughout the whole trip. The Avalanche Lake Trailhead is near the west entrance of the park, just past Lake McDonald.

The path to the lake starts with the Trail of the Cedars, which winds through old cedars and hemlock forests. After this section, the trail climbs along Avalanche Creek and flattens out once you reach the lake. Rated as moderate, the hike is 5.9 miles out and back.

Best Time to Visit: The best time to visit Avalanche Lake is between June and October.

Pass/Permit/Fees: The summer rate is $35 per vehicle, and the winter rate is $25 per vehicle.

Closest City or Town: West Glacier

Physical Address: Glacier National Park, 64 Grinnell Drive, West Glacier, MT 59936

GPS Coordinates: 48.6553° N, 113.7870° W

Did You Know? Avalanche Lake is fed almost entirely from the streams created by the melting snow and ice from Sperry Glacier.

Going-to-the-Sun Road

One of the most beautiful drives in the U.S., Going-to-the-Sun Road is certainly the most scenic drive in Glacier National Park. There are numerous places where you can stop and enjoy the views on this spectacular 50-mile mountain road.

There are also various hikes along the way, such as the Avalanche Trail. At 4 miles out and back, this trail has a gentle elevation and takes you to a pristine alpine lake. Other notable trails include the Highline Trail, Trail of Cedars, Hidden Lake Lookout, and St. Mary Falls Trail.

Best Time to Visit: The best time to visit Going-to-the-Sun Road is between early July to mid-October.

Pass/Permit/Fees: A Park Pass costs $35 for cars and $30 for motorcycles. An entry reservation ticket is also required for part of the year at a cost of $2.

Closest City or Town: West Glacier

Physical Address: Glacier National Park, 64 Grinnell Drive, West Glacier, MT 59936

GPS Coordinates: St. Mary Visitors Center (east): 48.4451° N, 113.2621° W; Apgar Visitor Center (west): 48.5231° N, 113.9885° W

Did You Know? This road appears in the opening credits of the horror film *The Shining*.

Upper Two Medicine Lake

Nestled in a U-shaped glacial valley, Upper Two Medicine Lake is in the southeastern corner of Glacier National Park. From the trailhead, it is around 10 miles round trip to the lake. Many choose the option of boating on the Sinopah to the west end of the Two Medicine Lake, hiking the remaining 1.9 miles to Upper Medicine Lake, and then returning 4.4 miles via the North Shore Trail.

The South Shore Trail starts at the Two Medicine parking lot near the boat dock and runs 5.5 miles one way. The North Shore Trail is 4.4 miles one way and begins near the camping ground parking lot at Pray Lake.

Best Time to Visit: The best time to visit Upper Two Medicine Lake is during the summer.

Pass/Permit/Fees: The summer rate is $35 per vehicle, and the winter rate is $25 per vehicle. Boat tickets are $16.75 for adults and $8.25 for children ages 4 to 12.

Closest City or Town: West Glacier

Physical Address: Upper Two Medicine Lake Campground, East Glacier Park, MT 59434

GPS Coordinates: 48.4692° N, 113.4472° W

Did You Know? The rock in the area is red because it contains Grinnell argillite. The red color is created from the reaction of oxygen and iron, creating rust in the sediment deposited in the water of the ancient Belt Sea.

Waterton-Glacier International Peace Park

This park is the union of Waterton Lakes National Park in Canada with Glacier National Park in Montana. The union is a World Heritage Site, and each park has been declared a biosphere reserve by UNESCO. The landscape is similar in the two parks, which are full of giant mountains, glaciers, expansive prairies, and thick forests.

Logan Pass is part of the Continental Divide and the highest point in Glacier National Park that's accessible by car. Two popular hiking trails start here: Hidden Lake Overlook Trail is 2.8 miles and easy-moderate, while Highline Trail is 11.6 miles and moderate.

Best Time to Visit: The best time to visit Waterton-Glacier International Peace Park is between June and September.

Pass/Permit/Fees: You must have your passport to cross the U.S.–Canada border.

Closest City or Town: West Glacier

Physical Address: Glacier National Park, 64 Grinnell Drive, West Glacier, MT 59936

GPS Coordinates: 48.6874° N, 113.8051° W

Did You Know? In 1932, this International Peace Park became the first in the world. It's a symbol of peace and goodwill between Canada and the United States.

Lake McDonald

Gouged out by glaciers from the Ice Age and surrounded by mountains, Lake McDonald is the largest lake in Glacier National Park at 10 miles long and nearly 500 feet wide. The lake sits within a valley that offers spectacular sights, trails, and waterfalls.

There are several ways to explore the area, such as hiking, kayaking, and canoeing. A scenic boat tour on the historic vessel *DeSmet* is also an option for travelers. Apgar Village is a famous location along the lake because of its colorful pebble beach and pristine view of the mountain range across the lake, and many visitors enjoy a stay at the rustic Lake McDonald Lodge.

Best Time to Visit: The best time to visit Lake McDonald is between June and October.

Pass/Permit/Fees: Summer rates are $35 for cars, $30 for motorcycles, and $20 for individuals. Winter rates are $25 for vehicles, $20 for motorcycles, and $15 for individuals.

Closest City or Town: Whitefish

Physical Address: Glacier National Park, 64 Grinnell Drive, West Glacier, MT 59936

GPS Coordinates: 48.5886° N, 113.9252° W

Did You Know? It is commonly thought that the name McDonald came from a trader named Duncan McDonald, whose name was carved in a nearby tree in 1878.

Stumptown Ice Den

The Stumptown Ice Den is the only rink in Montana that offers ice skating all year. More than 1,000 adults and children participate in the Ice Den's hockey and figure skating programs, and over 75,000 people visit the rink each year. Numerous figure skating and hockey camps that are hosted by the rink attract attendees from all over the U.S. and Canada.

There is even an NHL hockey prospect camp that serves as a scouting event for the National Hockey League. Public skating sessions are also available all year, and many people visit the Ice Den in the summer just to escape the heat.

Best Time to Visit: Times vary for public skate sessions, so check the Stumptown Ice Den's online calendar to find one that works for you.

Pass/Permit/Fees: Public skating sessions are $7 for everyone over the age of 5. Children ages 5 and under are free. Skate rentals are $3 per person.

Closest City or Town: Whitefish

Physical Address: 715 Wisconsin Avenue, Whitefish, MT 59937

GPS Coordinates: 48.4239° N, 114.3400° W

Did You Know? For many years, the Stumptown Ice Den was only a seasonal operation, but demand for ice time led to its year-round hours.

Whitefish Depot

The Whitefish Depot was constructed in 1928 as a stop on the Great Northern Railroad. It was designed in an alpine style to echo the resort hotels in nearby Glacier National Park. The cedar-shingled roof, three dormers, intricate stickwork, and carved brackets that support the roof's overhang make the building a work of art in its own right.

Service at the depot was discontinued in the 1980s, but the Stumptown Historical Society pledged to preserve the structure and renovate it to showcase the railroading history of Whitefish and the surrounding region. In addition, the depot's first floor is shared by Amtrak, which provides passenger service to nearly 35,000 riders per year.

Best Time to Visit: The Whitefish Depot is open daily from 6:00 a.m. to 2:00 p.m. and again from 4:00 p.m. to 11:30 p.m.

Pass/Permit/Fees: There is no fee to visit.

Closest City or Town: Whitefish

Physical Address: 500 Depot Street, Whitefish, MT 59937

GPS Coordinates: 48.4141° N, 114.3360° W

Did You Know? Amtrak built a 1,200-foot-long platform at the depot in 2011. It features an electric snow-melting system and platform lighting.

Whitefish Lake

At an elevation of 2,999 feet and surrounded by tall, forested mountains, Whitefish Lake is one of Montana's most popular lake destinations. A natural lake of around 5.2 square miles with about 15.9 miles of shoreline, Whitefish Lake is great for fishing, kayaking, and boating.

You can camp, boat, and swim at the Whitefish Lake State Park, and there are 25 campsites with both tent-only and RV spots. The three primary public access points along the lake are at Whitefish Lake State Park, Les Mason Park, and City Beach.

Best Time to Visit: The best time to visit Whitefish Lake is during the summer.

Pass/Permit/Fees: The day-use entry fee is $8 for vehicles and $4 for walk-ins, bicycles, or bus passengers. Montana residents who pay the $9 state park fee with their vehicle registration don't have to pay daily entrance fees.

Closest City or Town: Whitefish

Physical Address: Whitefish Lake State Park, 1615 W. Lakeshore Drive, Whitefish, MT 59937

GPS Coordinates: 48.4246° N, 114.3693° W

Did You Know? Many residents of the Whitefish area who are not on city water pull their drinking water directly from the lake, so it's an important community resource.

Lewis and Clark Caverns State Park

Montana's first state park features some of the largest known limestone caverns in the Northwest. These caverns are naturally air conditioned and lined with stalactites, stalagmites, helictites, and columns that are electrically lighted and safe to visit.

Access to the caverns is by guided tour only. The easy 1-mile Paradise Tour takes about 1.5 hours to complete. Along with the caverns, there are hiking trails to explore above ground and a campground. The diverse trail system spans 10 miles. Options range from easy strolls to demanding uphill climbs.

Best Time to Visit: The best time to visit Lewis and Clark Caverns State Park is between May and September.

Pass/Permit/Fees: Admission is $15 for visitors ages 15 and up or $10 for seniors, children ages 5 to 14, and disabled visitors.

Closest City or Town: Whitehall

Physical Address: Lewis and Clark Caverns State Park, 25 Lewis & Clark Caverns Road, Whitehall, MT 59759

GPS Coordinates: 45.8231° N, 111.8496° W

Did You Know? Despite its name, Lewis and Clark did not actually discover the caverns of this park. They did, however, traverse the wilderness in the area, and hikers can take in the same views they did on one of the multi-use trails in the park.

Castle Ghost Town

The town of Castle was created in the late 1800s during the height of the silver rush. The North Carolina Mine became the first in 1884, and there were 991 silver mines in the area by 1891. Castle's population peaked at 2,000 residents a few years later. A school, several stores, a few fraternal organizations, 7 brothels, 14 saloons, and a jail were built to support the growth.

The most famous resident of Castle was Martha Jane Cannary Burke, better known as Calamity Jane. In the 1890s, Calamity Jane came to Castle to open a restaurant, but that didn't last long because she and her husband were arrested just three weeks into their venture for not paying someone for a team of horses they had in their possession. In 1893, the silver panic sent residents fleeing from towns like Castle, leaving them totally abandoned by the 1930s.

Best Time to Visit: The best time to visit Castle Ghost Town is during the summer when the weather is warmer.

Pass/Permit/Fees: There is no fee to visit, but permission is required for access.

Closest City or Town: White Sulphur Springs

Physical Address: Meagher County Visitor Center, 14 W. Main Street, White Sulphur Springs, MT 59645

GPS Coordinates: 46.4439° N, 110.6707° W

Did You Know? Visitors to Castle can see the open rock basement of the general store and post office.

Smith River

This adventure by water on the Smith River, a tributary of the Missouri River, is a great opportunity for fly fishing and floating in a remote setting. Full of great scenery, the river flows for over 50 miles without any highways and then travels into a canyon. The river flows through private land, and accessing it can be difficult.

A popular spot to get in is at Camp Baker Fishing Access Site, and most floating occurs from Camp Baker to Eden Bridge Access Site.

Best Time to Visit: The best time to visit Smith River is during the spring and summer.

Pass/Permit/Fees: A permit is required for all recreational floating. Nine float parties are allowed on the river on any given day, and permits allow up to 4-day floats. To get a floating permit, you must apply to the Montana Fish, Wildlife, and Parks in February with a $10 nonrefundable fee. Permits are $15 for residents ages 6 to 12, $25 for residents over the age of 13, and $60 for nonresidents over the age of 13.

Closest City or Town: White Sulphur Springs

Physical Address: Camp Baker Smith River, Smith River Road, White Sulphur Springs, MT 59645

GPS Coordinates: 46.8079° N, 111.1826° W

Did You Know? Smith River is a nationally recognized recreational fishery and is especially known for its wild trout.

Proper Planning

With this guide, you are well on your way to properly planning a marvelous adventure. When you plan your travels, you should become familiar with the area, save any maps to your phone for access without internet, and bring plenty of water—especially during the summer months. Depending on which adventure you choose, you will also want to bring snacks or even a lunch. For younger children, you should do your research and find destinations that best suit your family's needs. You should also plan when and where to get gas, local lodgings, and food. We've done our best to group these destinations based on nearby towns and cities to help make planning easier.

Dangerous Wildlife

There are several dangerous animals and insects you may encounter while hiking. With a good dose of caution and awareness, you can explore safely. Here are steps you can take to keep yourself and your loved ones safe from dangerous flora and fauna while exploring:

- Keep to the established trails.
- Do not look under rocks, leaves, or sticks.
- Keep hands and feet out of small crawl spaces, bushes, covered areas, or crevices.
- Wear long sleeves and pants to keep arms and legs protected.
- Keep your distance should you encounter any dangerous wildlife or plants.

Limited Cell Service

Do not rely on cell service for navigation or emergencies. Always have a map with you and let someone know where you are and how long you intend to be gone, just in case.

First Aid Information

Always travel with a first aid kit in case of emergencies.

Here are items you should be certain to include in your primary first aid kit:

- Nitrile gloves
- Blister care products
- Band-Aids in multiple sizes and waterproof type
- Ace wrap and athletic tape
- Alcohol wipes and antibiotic ointment
- Irrigation syringe
- Tweezers, nail clippers, trauma shears, safety pins
- Small zip-lock bags containing contaminated trash

It is recommended to also keep a secondary first aid kit, especially when hiking, for more serious injuries or medical emergencies. Items in this should include:

- Blood clotting sponges
- Sterile gauze pads
- Trauma pads

- Second-skin/burn treatment
- Triangular bandages/sling
- Butterfly strips
- Tincture of benzoin
- Medications (ibuprofen, acetaminophen, antihistamine, aspirin, etc.)
- Thermometer
- CPR mask
- Wilderness medicine handbook
- Antivenin

There is much more to explore, but this is a great start.

For information on all national parks, visit https://www.nps.gov/index.htm .

This site will give you information on up-to-date entrance fees and how to purchase a park pass for unlimited access to national and state parks. This site will also introduce you to all of the trails at each park.

Always check before you travel to destinations to make sure there are no closures. Some hiking trails close when there is heavy rain or snow in the area and other parks close parts of their land for the migration of wildlife. Attractions may change their hours or temporarily shut down for various reasons. Check the websites for the most up-to-date information.

Made in the USA
Las Vegas, NV
01 November 2023

80014141R00079